Red Hat Society

Playful Paper Projects
& Party Ideas

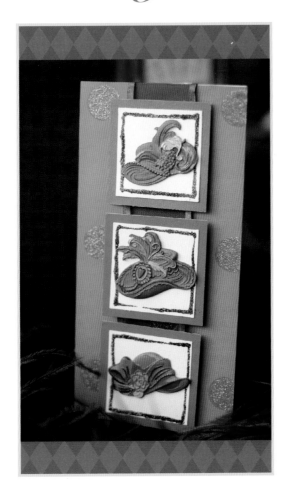

Red Hat Society

Playful Paper Projects
& Party Ideas

By Ruby RedHat

Sterling Publishing Co., Inc. New York
A Sterling /Chapelle Book

Chapelle, Ltd.:
Jo Packham, Sara Toliver, Cindy Stoeckl

If you have any questions or comments, please contact:
Chapelle, Ltd.,
P.O. Box 9252,
Ogden, UT 84409
(801) 621-2777 • (801) 621-2788 Fax
e-mail: chapelle@chapelleltd.com
Web site: www.chapelleltd.com

A Red Lips 4 Courage Book
Red Lips 4 Courage Communications, Inc.
8502 E. Chapman Ave., 303
Orange, CA 92869
Web site: www.redlips4courage.com

Library of Congress Cataloging-in-Publication Data available
10 9 8 7 6 5 4 3 2 1
Published by Sterling Publishing Co., Inc.
387 Park Ave. South, New York, NY 10016
©2006 by Ruby RedHat
Distributed in Canada by Sterling Publishing
c/o Canadian Manda Group, 165 Dufferin St.
Toronto, Ontario, Canada M6K 3H6
Distributed in the United Kingdom by GMC Distribution Services,
Castle Place, 166 High Street, Lewes, East Sussex, England BN7 1XU
Bramley Road, London W10 6SP, England
Distributed in Australia by Capricorn Link (Australia) Pty. Ltd.

P.O. Box 704, Windsor, NSW 2756, Australia
Printed and Bound in China
All Rights Reserved

Sterling ISBN-13: 978-1-4027-3204-1
        ISBN-10: 1-4027-3204-X

For information about custom editions, special sales, premium and
corporate purchases, please contact Sterling Special Sales Department
at (800) 805-5489; or e-mail: specialsales@sterlingpub.com.

Welcome

It started with a poem about women growing old
And donning hats of brilliant red to wear with hearts of gold.

A special friend received one at her birthday celebration
So much fun was had that day; there was such jubilation!

One by one, as birthdays came and a new friend turned age 50
Each one received a hat of red, and each thought it was nifty.

With purple outfits adding spark to chapeaux all in red
Huge throngs of women joined the fun with hats atop their heads.

My name is Ruby RedHat, yes it's true that I am small
But I can write, rhyme, party, play—yes, I can do it all!

Somewhere along the way they say I sprang up on the scene
Somehow I just took shape and form on a computer screen.

I think it's time to write a book just filled with inspiration
A book with notes, cards, pretty tags, and witty invitations.

Don't say you're not creative, there are none who can't create
Get out the glue and scissors, just jump in and you'll do great!

—Ruby RedHat

Table of Contents

Introduction

By now the story of the humble beginnings of the Red Hat Society has been told so many times it's becoming old hat. Not everyone would want to be called old hat, but for some of us, it's a compliment. A quick look through a trusty dictionary defines old hat as antique, out of fashion. If taken the wrong way, it makes old sound bad or even worse—boring. Some of my favorite hats are old. And in fact some of my dearest friends could be described as heading that way too. Yet, my hats and my friends are very much in fashion. Just look around the next time you are out and about. We seem to be everywhere these days. We are there in our red hats—often vintage, and dashingly coordinated with vivid purple attire.

In just a few years, membership in the Red Hat Society has blossomed into more than 1 million members. I knew I liked the idea of a sisterhood, but I never could have imagined so many others would too. We have connected through gatherings, or hatterings as I like to call them, at big and small community events, online, and through the mail. The connections we have made with each other is the essence of the Red Hat Society.

Without the camaraderie, who would there be to play with?

It usually starts with a self-appointed Queen, the best kind, don't you think? She spreads the word and calls others together to form a chapter. Often she uses an invitation or a

card. When the group gathers, inevitably someone gets creative and insists on crafting place cards, name tags, and a favor or two. A spark is lit and there are proclamations, poems, centerpieces, and mascots, which then lead to more invitations and cards, and, well, you get the idea.

I marvel every day at how many bins of mail come my way from imaginative Red Hatters. Creative cards and notes are filled with news of luncheons, hoots, coincidences, and happy synchronicities that all came about because we have communicated, connected with each other, and found a common bond.

Rarely do I get a note or letter that hasn't been either handmade or embellished in some way. Our sisterhood has taken to heart the battle cry to Ban Boring! Colorful papers, rhinestones, feathers, glitter, and drawings are used to make memories.

We are all artists in our own way. The artist in me can imagine the fun the sender must have had creating these communiqués. For many of us it's been too many years since we felt the fun of playing with crayons, glue, colored papers, and little doodads. There is something about being old hat that gives us a license to rediscover fun. Somewhere along the line, we got away from the fun of experimenting with creativity.

Remember making pictures with dyed macaroni? How about making stained glass windows with cardboard and tissue paper? Did you ever use crayons to color a paper different colors, which was then covered with black crayon and parts of the black areas were scraped away to make a picture?

The best part of these projects was proudly presenting them as a gift to my mother or father. Things aren't really any different with the cards, invitations, poems, and artwork we get at Hatquarters. Small

9

paper projects are fun and easy, and can make all the difference in how our sentiments are conveyed to a dear friend. How wonderful it is to look forward to a luncheon or hattering when the invitation is fun and enticing. Menu cards, favor boxes, and even the thank you note sent the next day all add to the personal experience of coming together. That's what sparked the idea that we should share some of the best ideas we've seen. And who better than the Red Hat Society's offical mascot, Ruby RedHat, to whip up such colorful and creative projects.

I am so excited about this book because it's filled with endless ideas for all kinds of invitations, cards, announcements (of a proper reduation, of course), favors, and hat decorations. Some of my personal favorites are the great ideas for customizing and embellishing our playing cards. These become little pieces of art to be traded and treasured. What a great way to remember the special sisters we meet at our hoots and hatterings.

These projects are photographed in settings overflowing with ideas for your next get-together. Whether it's lemonade or something a little stronger in the sugar-rimmed glass, who can resist the temptation of at least a sip? Ruby RedHat dances her way through a reduation, picnic, birthday, and some "just because" gatherings.

We are such busybodies and we seem to want to know what other Red Hatters are doing. Ruby keeps a little journal—and in her case it was indeed little—of some of the antics she has witnessed in her travels. We convinced her to let us edit them a bit, as she tends to ramble on, and let us share them with you.

In order to ensure the utmost fun when working on any of these projects, you must remember the red rule: "The rules are, there are no rules." If you don't feel like cutting, tear. If you don't feel like gluing, tape. If you don't like the color, change it. Do as you please, just please do have fun.

And never forget that personal touches make all the difference in how we come together to play.

Yours in Happy Hatting,

Sue Ellen Cooper

Exalted Queen Mother

Years ago, I was feeling a bit stifled in my role as chief cook and bottle washer and realized that one of the things I really missed was drawing and painting. When I listened to that inner voice and finally plunged myself into my art, I began to feel the sense of joy and personal happiness that comes from doing something you love. The spirit and elation that the Red Hat Society has brought me has become a favorite subject of my work. I am generally a little shy about sharing, but since I'm encouraging you to take the time for creative fun, I thought I'd show you some of the things I have enjoyed drawing on pages 8-11.

Sue Ellen Cooper

Tools & Techniques

*B*efore you get started on any of the projects featured on the following pages, you must first do one very important thing: Toss out all ideas of perfection and get serious about an anything-but-conservative approach. Brighter, sillier, and gaudy are better in our book. When it comes to Red Hatters, red and purple reign supreme and our younger sisters have lavender and pink to live by.

Today's craft and hobby stores are filled with these vibrant hues. From scrapbooking supplies and boas to buttons and beads to, well, just about anything else you can think to make and embellish a card, bag, or tag can be found.

I love to play with scissors, glue, tape, stamps, stickers, embellishments, paper scraps, and trims. I may be amid a mess of supplies, but I am always having a ball. This section covers the materials I use and the techniques (or lack of!) that readers will need to complete the projects featured throughout this book.

Tools

Adhesives (A)

- Acid-free adhesive
- Foam dots
- Glue dots
- Glue sticks
- Masking tape
- Spray adhesive

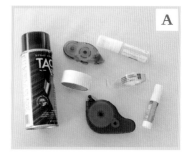

Coloring Tools (B, C)

- Chalk
- Colored pencils
- Colored pens
- Crayons
- Inkpads
- Water pens
- Watercolors

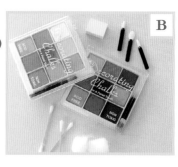

Chapter 1

Cutting Tools (D)

- Craft mat
- Deckle-edge scissors
- Exacto knife
- Paper cutter
- Straight-edge scissors

Embossing Tools (F)

- Embossing inkpad
- Embossing powder
- Heat tool
- Pen
- Tray

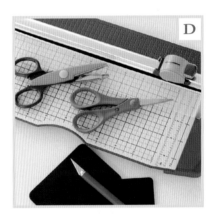

Embellishments (E)

- Beads
- Buttons
- Craft wire
- Fibers
- Waxy flax

Eyelet Setting Tools (G)

- Craft mat
- Eyelet hole punch
- Eyelet setter
- Eyelet tweezers
- Eyelets
- Hammer setting tool

Hole Punches (H)

In addition to traditional metal punches that create small holes, larger hole punches are available in a variety of shapes, such as tags.

Laminating Machine (I)

Paper Crimper (J)

Scrapbooking Paper (K)

Striping Tools (L)

- Ink roller
- Paintbrush
- Sponge brayer
- Sponges
- Stripe stencil
- Water brush

Stickers (M)

Additional Materials

- Computer and printer
- Embroidery needle
- Glitter
- Piercing tool
- Rubber stamps and inkpads
- Sandpaper
- Sticker machine

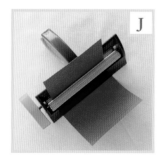

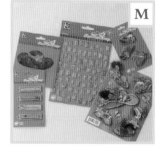

Adding Brads

*W*hen layering two or more papers, a decorative way to accomplish this is to add brads. To begin, make small slit in papers with safety pin or piercing tool (A). Pick up one brad at a time and place brad in slit (B). Push through and secure at back (C). Repeat on other side (D).

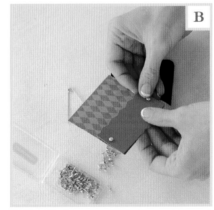

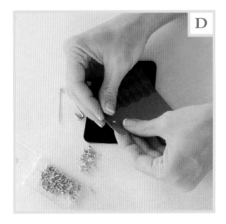

Distressing

*B*efore you begin the distressing technique, lay your paper flat (A). Tear one side of paper (B) then sand surface of paper lightly with sandpaper (C).

Roll up paper loosely (D), crumple paper (E), then unroll (F). Crush paper (G) then flatten (H), and you've got the final aged look.

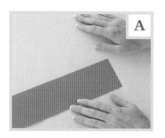
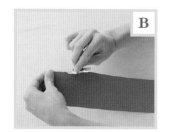

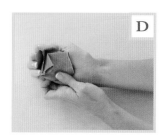

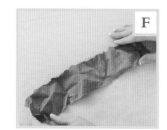

Embossing

*S*tamp image of choice with embossing inkpad then sprinkle on embossing powder over tray (I). Carefully return excess powder to container (J).

Shake off excess and be sure all loose powder has been removed (K). Hold heat gun several inches from paper to set (L).

Glittering

*W*rite name or message on paper of choice with an adhesive pen designed for rub-on applications (A). You can write freehand with this type of pen. Pick up glitter with finger and rub glitter over letters (B) until letters are covered with glitter (C). Shake off excess glitter and you have finished project (D). You can also stamp designs with embossing ink then sprinkle on glitter.

  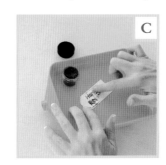 

Making a Tag

*T*o cut your own tag, place template on paper of your choice and trace with pencil (E). Trace additional tag shapes if desired. Hold paper in one hand and scissors in the other and cut (F). Cut desired size (G) then trim any uneven edges (H). Punch hole on top if desired.

Personalizing Stamps

*U*sing a removable alphabet letter rubber stamp, choose which letters and/or images you want to stamp and place on acrylic bar (A). Adhere where desired to create word or design in straight line or curved shape. Be sure stamps are firmly in place (B). Stamp on inkpad (C). Stamp on paper then remove to reveal words (D) or image. Let ink dry.

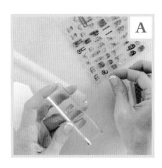
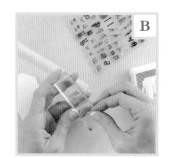

Punching a Tag

*P*lace tag punch where desired on paper of choice then press down firmly (E). Lift up tag punch and remove shape (F). Continue to punch (G) until desired number of shapes is obtained (H). Tags may be created out of cardstock or decorative paper.

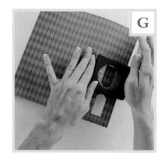

Setting Eyelets

*P*osition paper of choice on craft mat then punch hole with eyelet hole punch and hammer setting tool (A), making sure hole is proper size (B). Pick up eyelet with tweezers and place eyelet in hole (C). Place paper tag on craft mat with back side of paper and bottom of eyelet facing up (D) then pick up eyelet setter and place over eyelet (E). Using eyelet setter and hammer, set eyelet (F) then make sure eyelet is flat (G). If eyelet is not flat, reposition eyelet setter on eyelet then hammer again (H).

Sponging Edges

*T*o create decorative finished edge, you'll need a tag or paper of your choice, scrap paper, an inkpad, and a small sponge (A). Gently dip sponge in inkpad then wipe edge of tag (B). Continue wiping edge around tag then set on scrap paper to dry completely (C). Wipe off excess ink with dry part of sponge (D), or continue technique over surface of tag.

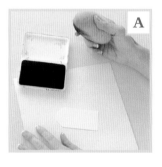

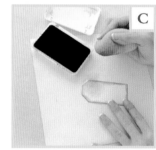

Water Brush Stamping

*P*ress rubber stamp of your choice firmly onto inkpad then stamp image on tag or paper of your choice (E). Press water pen tip to release water (F). Dip pen in inkpad, using lid to adjust amount of color (G). Using water brush, paint image (H). If more ink is needed, press down water brush again to release water then dip in inkpad.

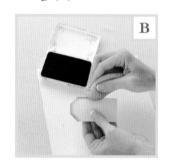

Stringing Wire

*C*hoose beading embellishments and ready craft wire (A). Unroll craft wire until desired length is reached (B). Cut wire then start stringing beads (C) and buttons (D), if desired. Continue in pattern of your choice (E) until desired length and look is achieved (F). Secure embellishments in place by wrapping wire around your smallest finger several times (G), creating a curlicue (H).

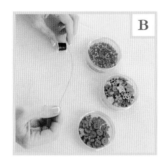

Chapter 2

We Take Time for Tease!

When we all get together, and we venture out to play
We dine, we laugh, we share—we find adventure every day.

We take our fancy cups of tea with sugar, lemon, and milk
We dress in cotton, linen, velvet, damask, or in silk.

Some friends are old, some friends are new, in purple and in red
We share so much together, with bright hats upon our heads.

We love to share a laugh or joke, and always love a pun
There are no regulations, just come prepared for fun.

Come gussied up, in this or that, in anything you please
Remember, always come for fun and be prepared to tease!

—Ruby RedHat

Tea Time Tag Card

Materials

- $1/2$" ribbon: purple
- 1" ribbon: sheer purple
- Acid-free adhesive
- Cardstock: lavender, white
- Decorative paper: red and purple patterned, red striped
- Fibers
- Hole punch
- Scissors
- Sequins: purple
- Stickers: alphabet letters, embossed tea-themed
- Vellum tag

Directions

Cut white cardstock and red striped decorative paper to $4^{1}/_{4}$" x $5^{1}/_{2}$". Adhere striped paper to white cardstock.

Cut white cardstock to $4^{1}/_{4}$" x $3^{1}/_{2}$". Cut red and purple decorative paper to $4^{1}/_{4}$" x $3^{1}/_{2}$"; adhere decorative paper to white cardstock.

Create pocket by gluing only along sides and bottom of striped decorative paper. Push down firmly and let dry completely.

Embellish pocket with $3/_{4}$" strip of lavender cardstock. Adhere row of sequins to strip. Add fibers and sticker to vellum tag, then adhere to center of strip.

To make tag, cut lavender cardstock to $2^{1}/_{4}$" x 5". Cut top of tag in desired shape; punch hole at top and add $7^{1}/_{4}$" lengths of both ribbons. Finish edges of ribbon by snipping them at angle. Decorate with stickers, spelling out Tea Time. Add tea-themed sticker and $1/_{2}$" strip of decorative paper underneath. Place tag inside pocket.

Well-Meaning Slip

After a delightful high tea, the Spicy Red Hat Chicks of SC (Fort Mill, South Carolina) headed back to their cars. While walking, one of the Red Hatters felt something unusual around her ankles. She looked down and noticed it was her slip, its elastic band broken. Rather than engaging in a fit of embarrassment, she just stepped out of the slip and swung it around her head, singing, "Hi Yo Silver!"

Doily Menu Card

Materials

- ¼" ribbon: sheer purple
- Acid-free adhesive
- Cardstock: purple, white
- Decorative paper: red, red patterned
- Inkpad: purple
- Paper doily: white square
- Rubber stamp: small teapot
- Scissors
- Stickers: alphabet letters, purple floral

Directions

Cut and fold purple cardstock into 6" x 6" top-fold card. With stamp and inkpad, randomly stamp teapot all over front of card.

Cut square doily to fit front of card as desired. Cut red decorative paper to fit under doily and adhere both on front of card.

Cut red patterned decorative paper into 4½" x 2½" rectangle. Adhere to top center edge of card front. Cut white cardstock into 4" x 2" rectangle. Adhere on top of red patterned decorative paper, centered within the space.

Add Menu alphabet letters to center of white cardstock and purple floral stickers to each corner. Tie ribbon into bow at top fold.

The details set the tone for a party. This red doily menu is a festive yet elegant way to present your food choices.

Doily Tease Invitation

Materials

- $\frac{1}{2}$" button: red
- Acid-free adhesive
- Cardstock: purple, white
- Fibers: purple
- Inkpad: red
- Paper doily: red
- Rubber stamps: alphabet letters, gift tag
- Scissors
- Stickers: border design, tea-themed embossed

Directions

Cut purple cardstock to 5" x 7". Stamp tags onto white cardstock; cut out. Using red inkpad, stamp words Time for Tease and date using alphabet stamps.

Attach tea sticker to bottom left corner, border sticker across bottom, and both tags at top of card.

Thread 2" lengths of fibers through button; adhere both to top tag. Cut out doily edges and adhere to back of card.

Lacy doilies dress up this invitation made with purple cardstock. Letters can be drawn on or created using a customized stencil.

Tea Invite with Vellum Envelope

Materials

- Acid–free adhesive
- Cardstock: purple, white
- Computer and printer
- Embroidery needle
- Hole punch
- Inkpad: purple
- Piercing tool
- Rubber stamp: teapot
- Scissors
- Vellum paper: patterned
- Waxy flax: purple, red

Directions

For envelope: Cut and fold vellum into 6" bottom-fold shape. Cut small U-shaped notch on top of one side. Adhere only side edges together.

For invite: Print information from computer onto white cardstock; cut to 5" square. Cut purple cardstock into 5¼" square. Layer white cardstock on front of purple cardstock, centered.

With purple inkpad, stamp teapot image lightly in center of white cardstock. Using piercing tool, pierce two sets of holes evenly down each side of card. Using embroidery needle, sew red waxy flax through pierced holes to create crisscrossed effect. Punch hole at top; thread two 6" pieces of red waxy flax and two 6" pieces of purple waxy flax through hole and tie in knot.

To create this crisscross design on the invitation I wove through long pieces of red waxy flax.

Votive Name Card

Materials

- Acid-free adhesive
- Cardstock: beige
- Decorative paper: purple patterned
- Fine-point felt-tip pens: black, red
- Glue dots
- Hole punch
- Paper crimper
- Scissors
- Tag punch
- Votive candle: red
- Waxy flax: red, natural, purple

Directions

Cut ³/₄" strip of beige cardstock to fit around candle; crimp with paper crimper. *Note:* Crimping will shrink the paper, so make the strip a little longer than you think you need to wrap around the votive.

Cut ¹/₄" strip of decorative paper to fit around candle. Adhere to center of beige cardstock with adhesive. Wrap two layers of paper around center of candle and secure with glue dots.

Punch tag out of beige cardstock. Write name and outline edge of tag with black and red pens. Punch hole at top of tag then tie onto votive using three 14" strands of waxy flax (one of each color).

Everyone will want to take their seat when they spy their name on a cute place card they can carry home after the party.

Let's Do Tea Card

Materials

- ¼" ribbons: pink, purple, red
- Acid-free adhesive
- Cardstock: pink, purple, red, white
- Decorative paper: red swirls
- Fine-point felt-tip pen: black
- Hole punches: 1 small, 1 large
- Scissors
- Scrapbook frame

Directions

Cut and fold cardstock into 5½" x 4¼" top-fold card. Cut bottom 1¼" off card front.

Glue 1¾" strip of red swirls decorative paper to inside bottom of card. Write invitation information inside card.

Punch various circles from pink, purple, and red cardstock; glue to front of card in random fashion.

Layer small square of red swirls decorative paper behind scrapbook frame. Write Let's Do Tea on red square. With small hole punch, make five evenly spaced holes at bottom edge of front of card. Attach set of three brightly colored knotted ribbons through each hole.

Party details can be printed using a computer or you can use alphabet letter stamps.

Teacup Card

Reduation Tea
In honor of
Betty Crawford

Tuesday, March 11th
3:00 p.m.
Piccadilly Inn
2527 Main St.

Materials

- Acid-free adhesive
- Brad: pink
- Computer and printer
- Decorative paper: lavender patterned
- Paper: pink, white
- Pink hat charm
- Scissors
- Sequins: pink
- Stickers: hat, floral

Directions

Cut teacup out of decorative paper using Teacup template (page 136). Print out tea information for inside of card on white paper; cut out and adhere to inside of teacup card.

Fold pink paper into small envelope shape. Adhere tag decorated with stickers and a brad to back of envelope. Adhere both to front of teacup card. Personalize tags for the invitee. Adhere sequins to front of card.

Party details can be written on the inside of the invite or printed out using your computer.

Glove Invitation

Materials

- ¼" ribbon: red
- ½" ribbon: white
- Acid-free adhesive
- Decorative paper: red floral, purple harlequin
- Fine-point felt-tip pen: black
- Glue dots
- Rhinestones: red
- Scissors
- Sticker: border

Think Pink

Members of the Red Hot Hatties (Topeka, Kansas), all grandmothers, decided to hold a Pink & Pretty Tea for their granddaughters, ages 2-16. The girls decorated their own pink hats, played Pin a Feather on the Red Hat, and sang a new Pink Hat song made up by some of the girls. Everyone ate finger sandwiches in cookie cutter designs, crackers and cheese cut into shapes, peanut butter and jelly sandwiches rolled up and sliced, and fancy veggies including radish roses, onion chrysanthemums, and curled celery. Pink lemonade in teapots was served and the newly anointed Pink Hatters painted their fingernails pink and lavender.

Directions

Trace glove using your own hand, fingers together, on red floral paper; cut out. Mark lines for finger separations using black pen. Cut red ribbon to fit across bottom of glove; add rhinestones across ribbon.

Add border sticker to bottom edge of glove, about 1½" from bottom. Cut purple harlequin paper to 4" x 5"; fold into fan shape. Tie white ribbon in bow around bottom of fan.

Write invitation details on back of glove. Using glue dots, position fan near thumb and fold thumb over, as if it were holding onto fan.

While this glove is two sided, you can easily create a card that opens by simply cutting the template on a folded piece of cardstock. Be sure that the thumb is at the right, away from the fold. This is a great project for teas or theater invites!

Thank You For Tea Card

Materials

- ½" gingham ribbon: black and white
- Acid-free adhesive
- Cardstock: lavender, purple, white
- Decorative paper: red swirls
- Foam squares
- Glue dots
- Inkpad: lavender
- Rubber stamp: floral
- Scissors
- Sticker: embossed tea-themed

Directions

Cut and fold white cardstock into 4 ¼" x 5 ½" side-fold card. Stamp floral image over front of card.

Using Frame template (page 139), lavender cardstock, and red swirls paper, cut two layers of frames, one slightly larger than the other. Layer frames with glue dots then add purple cardstock on top.

Attach ribbon down front of card with glue dots. Attach frames to front of card; adhere sticker in center of layered frames with foam squares.

I layered my frames, adding glue dots between each layer for a dimensional effect.

Laminated Name Tag

Materials

- ¼" ribbon: color of your choice
- Acid-free adhesive
- Cardstock: purple
- Decorative paper: red swirls
- Laminating machine
- Paper flowers: lavender, purple
- Pencil
- Pin back
- Rhinestones
- Scissors
- Stickers: alphabet letters
- Tag template

Directions

Trace tag template on red swirls paper and cut out. Trace red swirls tag on purple cardstock; cut out slightly larger. Adhere red swirls tag to top of purple cardstock.

Decorate front of red swirls paper card with alphabet stickers, paper flowers, rhinestones, and ribbon at the edge. Laminate and let set at least 10 minutes. Adhere pin back to tag.

The best way to deal with pesky memory blips is to agree that you'll all wear a festive name tag when you gather. By laminating the tag, you can wear it over and over again.

Teacup Door Hanger

Materials

- Acid-free adhesive
- Cardstock: white
- Decorative paper: coordinating patterns, 2
- Inkpads: purple, red
- Pencil
- Rubber stamps: alphabet letters, assorted tea themed
- Scissors
- Shredded paper: your color of choice
- Tea bags

Directions

Copy Teacup Door Hanger template (page 138) onto white cardstock; cut out. Cover door hanger with decorative paper.

Stamp wording and tea images on 3" square piece of white cardstock. Attach white square stamped with tea images to front of door hanger. Fill pocket with shredded paper, tea bags, and details about your tea party!

Hang this tag on your doorknob and you'll be telling friends you can be disturbed anytime for tea.

Tea Bag Card

Materials

- ¼" ribbon: red
- Acid-free adhesive
- Cardstock: white
- Decorative paper: purple, red plaid
- Exacto knife
- Hole punch
- Pencil
- Scissors
- Tape

Directions

Copy Tea Bag Card template (page 139) onto cardstock; cut out. Cut out teacup image at center using Exacto knife. Adhere decorative paper to front of cardstock. Tape tea bag to inside of card, positioning in center of teacup cutout. Punch two holes at top. String ribbon through holes and tie.

Going with the Float

When it comes to taking tea, some Red Hatters are ready any time, any place. The S.S. Sisters (Saybrook, Illinois) raised their teacups to celebrate a local "Freedom Fest" patriotic parade. They got into the spirit of the day dressed in their regalia—and drinking tea—on their Red Hat Society chapter float. Who says red and purple aren't patriotic colors!

The tea bag is securely in place by taping it to the inside of the project.

Chapter 3

We Have Merry Mirthdays!

Someone is having a birthday
She's sporting a purple hat
Her outfit is red
Because the queen said
On our birthdays we each should do that.

That means we have to go shopping,
To be ready to dress in reverse
For a purple chapeau
And some red that won't go
Perhaps some new shoes and a purse.

Now isn't it fun to be silly
In upside-down purple and red
This change once a year
Makes it perfectly clear
That birthdays are nothing to dread.

—Linda Murphy, Esteemed Vice-Mother

Folded Mirthday Card

Materials

- Acid-free adhesive
- Cardstock: purple, red, white
- Decorative paper: red-and-white checkered
- Fine-point felt-tip pen: black
- Inkpad: purple
- Rubber stamp: cupcake with candle
- Scissors

Directions

Cut and fold red cardstock to 8" x 4". Score cardstock 2" from each end. Cut two pieces of red-and-white checkered paper into envelope shape.

Attach checkered paper to 2" flaps of red cardstock on inside and fold over front of card. Accent edges with pen.

Cut white cardstock to 3³/₄" square; adhere to inside of card. Stamp white cardstock square with cupcake images and add birthday sentiment.

Cut 1" strip of purple cardstock to 8¹/₄"; wrap loosely around card. Cut white cardstock to 2" square; stamp with cupcake image and outline edge of square with black pen. Add white cardstock square to cover seam of purple strip.

There may have been days when we wanted to hide from our birthdays, but now they are Mirthdays and we celebrate in style. A folding card is easy to make, and is a wonderful way to show a Red Hat sister she is special.

Mirthday Gift Bag

Materials

- Acid-free adhesive
- Cardstock: white
- Fine-point felt-tip pen: black
- Gift bag: white, 4" x 5"
- Handmade paper: purple
- Hole punch
- Inkpads: black, purple, red
- Pencil
- Rubber stamps: shoes, stacked hatboxes
- Scissors
- Tag template
- Water brush
- Waxy flax: red

Directions

Randomly stamp gift bag with images of shoes, alternating red and purple ink. Stamp hatboxes image on 2" x 3" white cardstock with black ink.

Color in hatboxes with water brush, alternating purple and red inks. Tear handmade paper to about 3" x 4"; adhere to front of gift bag, then layer with image of hatboxes.

Trace tag template on white cardstock; cut out. Punch hole at side; brush edges with red ink and sponge, then tie to gift bag with waxy flax.

A fun tag and decorated gift bag will be as treasured as the gift itself. Once the Merry Mirthday has passed, the lucky Mirthday girl can use it to tote things to her next gathering.

Cake Tag & Gift Bag

Materials

- ³/₄" ribbon: red
- Acid-free adhesive
- Brads: metal star, 6
- Cardstock: lavender, purple, red
- Craft wire
- Eyelet: lavender
- Eyelet setting tools
- Gift bag: white
- Glitter: gold
- Inkpads: purple, red
- Rhinestones: pink, purple
- Rubber stamps: assorted circles and stars
- Scissors
- Sponge
- Sticker: birthday cake
- String: white
- Tag template
- Wire spiral clip: silver

Directions

To decorate front of gift bag: Cut red cardstock to 3" x length of bag; cut purple cardstock to 7 ¹/₂" x length of bag. Stamp assorted circles and stars with red ink on red card-stock, purple ink on purple cardstock. Adhere to front of bag. Embellish bag with star brads at top and bottom.

To make cake tag: Trace tag on lavender cardstock; cut out. Decorate tag with 2" band, torn on top and bottom. Cut white cardstock to 2" square. Rub edges of card with purple ink and sponge. Embellish with birthday cake, rhinestones, and glitter stars. Wrap craft wire around top of card several times; add wire spiral clip at top. Add small purple cardstock square to top of tag then layer white square; add eyelet at center. Tie tag to bag with string.

If you don't have an eyelet, just poke a small hole at the top to hang your tag.

Three Tags Card

Materials

- 1" button: purple
- Acid-free adhesive
- Cardstock: purple, white
- Decorative paper: red swirls
- Embroidery floss
- Eyelet setting tools
- Eyelets: purple, 3
- Glue dots
- Hat charms: 3 assorted
- Scissors
- Tags: 2 small, 1 medium

Directions

Cut and fold white cardstock into 7" x 5" top-fold card. Cut and adhere decorative paper to fit front of card.

Cut 3"-wide strip of purple cardstock to fit width of card; adhere to front of card. Set eyelet at top of each tag. Adhere tags to front of card.

Adhere hat charms to tags using glue dots. Add button tied with embroidery floss to lower right corner.

Some of us dream of a closet full of shoes; my fantasy is boxes filled with hats. A card like this doesn't have to be reserved for Mirthdays, and it's sure to make hat addicts smile.

hree Hats Card

Materials

- 1 ³/₄" sheer ribbon: purple
- Acid-free adhesive
- Cardstock: purple, red, white
- Decorative paper: red with purple glitter polka dots
- Glitter: purple
- Glitter glue
- Ribbon
- Scissors
- Stickers: various hats, 3

Directions

Cut and fold red cardstock into 3 ¹/₂" x 8" side-fold card. Cut and adhere decorative paper on front of card. Attach ribbon down front of card. (Fold over top and adhere on top of card inside.)

Layer white and purple cardstock to make three 2" squares. Outline edges of white squares with glitter glue. Let dry.

Rub purple glitter over dried glue. Attach hat stickers to center of each square, then adhere squares on top of ribbon.

You've heard about three heads being better than one?
Well three hats are even better, and cute cards prove it.

Friends Card

Materials

- Acid-free adhesive
- Beads: assorted, 4
- Cardstock: white
- Decorative paper: purple striped, red swirls
- Inkpads: green, pink, red
- Rubber stamp: wildflowers
- Scissors
- Sponge
- Waxy flax: red

Directions

Cut and fold cardstock into $5\frac{1}{2}$" x $4\frac{1}{4}$" side-fold card. Cut $1\frac{1}{2}$" off front flap; cut and adhere purple striped paper to fit front flap of card, tearing at right side. Cut and adhere $1\frac{1}{2}$" x $4\frac{1}{4}$" strip of red swirls papers to inside right edge of card.

Stamp flowers on $3\frac{1}{4}$" square of white cardstock with red and pink inks for flowers, green ink for stems. Rub edges of square with red ink and sponge. Adhere square to front of card. Thread beads onto waxy flax then tie around right-hand side of card.

There is never a shortage of friends when you are a Red Hatter, and a flower-embellished card for a special friend will always be welcomed and appreciated.

Girls Just Wanna Have Fun Tag & Box

Materials

- ¼" ribbon: purple
- Acid-free adhesive
- Beaded trim
- Cardstock: purple
- Decorative paper: light purple, purple striped, red with purple glitter polka dots
- Eyelet: red, 1
- Eyelet setting tools
- Feather: purple
- Gift box: top fold
- Glitter: red
- Glitter glue
- Inkpad: purple
- Pencil
- Ribbon rose: red
- Rubber stamp: Girls Just Wanna Have Fun
- Scissors
- Stickers: flowers, hat
- Tag template

Directions

Cover pre-made gift box with purple striped paper on top, red with purple glitter polka dots on bottom. Wrap paper around front corners and overlap on sides to give a nice, clean front. For top flap of box, glue striped paper larger than flap then trim paper to fit flap. Cut decorative band about 1½" wide and long enough to go around box. Layer with second decorative paper; adhere around box. Embellish center of band with feather and ribbon rose.

Trace tag template onto purple cardstock; cut out. Cut out second tag slightly smaller using light purple paper. Adhere to purple cardstock tag. Stamp Girls Just Wanna Have Fun on tag; embellish with stickers. Line outside edge of tag with glitter glue then sprinkle on glitter; let dry. Add eyelet to top of tag then tie tag onto box with ribbon. Adhere beaded trim along top edge of box.

This tag and box project is easy to embellish with glitter and beaded trim.

Lady in Waiting Card

Materials

- Acid-free adhesive
- Cardstock: lavender, purple, red, white
- Decorative paper: purple striped, red floral
- Eyelets: red flowers, 4
- Inkpads: black, lavender, red
- Metal embellishment
- Rickrack: red
- Rubber stamp: woman in dress
- Soft chalks: lavender, red

Directions

Cut and fold white cardstock into $3\frac{1}{2}$" x 8" side-fold card. Cut $1\frac{3}{4}$" x 4" rectangle out of purple cardstock and same out of red cardstock and decorative papers; adhere all to front of card. Add rickrack down center of card. Stamp woman in dress image on white cardstock and color in with chalk. Layer onto $2\frac{1}{2}$" x 5" piece of lavender cardstock. Set eyelet in each corner. Add metal embellishment. Attach to card front.

Our Lady in Waiting is more likely to be the member who gets there early and finds herself sitting and waiting for others.

ConREDulations!

Turning 50 may be a dreaded occasion for some, but when you have Red Hat sisters like the Red Hot Hootin' Nannies of Watts Bar (Ten Mile, Tennessee) it's not so bad. The Queen Mum, Her Imperial Highness, celebrated her reduation in Red Hat style with her younger sister and fellow chapterettes. Although her older sister couldn't make it to Tennessee for the festivities, she sent best wishes wrapped in a purple satin robe designed with a red hat emblem on the back.

Reduation Invitation

Materials

- ½" ribbon: red
- Acid-free adhesive
- Cardstock: purple, red, white
- Eyelet setting tools
- Eyelets: red, 4
- Hole punch
- Inkpad: red
- Rubber stamps: alphabet letters, numbers
- Scissors
- Sponge
- Sticker: hat

Directions

To make invitation holder: Trace 4" x 12" tag onto purple cardstock; cut out. Fold up 4" at bottom to create pocket; add eyelets to each corner. Cut white cardstock to 3" square and red cardstock slightly larger. Adhere white cardstock onto red cardstock then embellish with hat sticker. Adhere to front of pocket.

To make invitation: Trace tag template onto white cardstock; cut out. *Note:* Invite should be 1" smaller than invitation holder. Stamp invitation information on white tag. Punch hole at top of invite then tie red ribbon at top. Sponge edges with red ink. Insert invite into pocket.

Her big moment has arrived, and she can shed the pink hat and join the red brigade. Be sure the ceremony is as special as the new Red Hatter by extending a proper whimsical invitation to the event.

Wire Spiral Card

Materials

- Acid-free adhesive
- Cardstock: purple, red, white
- Eyelet setting tools
- Eyelets: purple, 3
- Scissors
- Stickers: border, three-dimensional hat
- Wire spiral clip: purple

Directions

Cut and fold red cardstock into 3" x 3" side-fold card. Cut purple cardstock to 2¾" square and white cardstock to 2½" square. Layer white cardstock on purple cardstock then adhere both to front of card.

Set three eyelets at bottom of card front. Accent side of card front with border sticker, three-dimensional hat, and metal spiral.

I always seem to be grabbing my purse, slipping into my scuffies, and flying out the door in a rush to a party. I like to have a few Red Hat cards on hand to fit any occasion.

Flower Pot Card

Materials

- ½" button: lavender
- Acid-free adhesive
- Cardstock: white
- Decorative paper: purple striped, red swirls
- Die cut: flower
- Foam square
- Glitter: green, irridescent
- Glitter glue
- Inkpad: green, lavender
- Pencil
- Scissors
- Sponge
- Waxy flax: purple

Directions

Draw flower pot on cardstock; cut out. Cut and adhere red swirls paper to front of card.

Sponge die cut leaves green and outer portion of flower purple; leave center white. Sprinkle on glitter; let dry. Tie waxy flax through button and knot on top; adhere to center of flower then adhere entire piece to front of card with foam square.

To make flower pot rim: Adhere purple striped paper to cardstock rim; adhere to top of flower pot. Print words on computer, layer onto cardstock, add glitter, and attach to card front.

There are no green thumbs necessary to plant a paper flower pot. It's simple to cut out the shape, and a sticker flower will always be in bloom.

Flower Card

Materials

- Acid-free adhesive
- Cardstock: red, white
- Decorative paper: coordinating papers, 2
- Eyelet setting tools
- Eyelets: red, 4
- Glitter: iridescent colors of your choice
- Glitter glue
- Hemp
- Inkpads: green, purple, red
- Paper crimper
- Rubber stamp: flower
- Scissors
- Sponge

Directions

Cut and fold white cardstock into 5 1/2" x 4 1/4" top-fold card. Cover front of card with decorative paper; trim edges.

Cut red cardstock to 3" x 3 1/4" rectangle; crimp with paper crimper then tear bottom of rectangle. Adhere to center of card.

Cut white cardstock to 2 3/4" x 2 1/4". Stamp flower using green and red ink; let dry. Embellish outline of flower with glitter then adhere to center of crimped paper. Sponge around flower with purple ink.

Set two eyelets on each side of flower. Tie hemp in knots through eyelets.

Adding a bit of glitter for shine gives the flowers on this card pizzazz, and makes it a welcome sparkle in any Pink Hatter's day.

Welcome Pink Hatters Card

Materials

- Acid-free adhesive
- Buttons: lavender, 3
- Cardstock: pink
- Decorative paper: lavender
- Glue dots
- Inkpad: purple
- Pink Hat lapel pin
- Rubber stamps: flower, Welcome
- Sandpaper
- Scissors

Directions

Cut and fold pink cardstock into $4\,\frac{1}{4}$" x $5\,\frac{1}{2}$" side-fold card. Stamp Welcome onto strip of lavender paper. Cut out $4\,\frac{1}{4}$" x $1\,\frac{3}{4}$" rectangle then adhere to bottom of card.

Sand piece of lavender paper. Cut to $1\,\frac{1}{4}$" x $3\,\frac{3}{4}$" then adhere to front of card.

Stamp flower onto another rectangle piece. Cut out 3" x $2\,\frac{1}{4}$" piece then adhere to card front.

Add buttons to strip of pink cardstock then adhere to bottom of card. Remove pin back from Pink Hat lapel pin then attach to card with glue dots.

Today's children are our future, and we must raise them to learn our ways. Make future Red Hat sisters welcome with a special greeting that acknowledges their youth.

Congrats Flap Card

A small piece of decorative paper, adhered with brads on each side, is ideal for holding a pair of tickets or a gift card.

Materials

- Acid-free adhesive
- Brads: lavender, 2
- Cardstock: lavender, white
- Decorative paper: coordinating patterns, 3
- Inkpad: black
- Pencil
- Rubber stamps: alphabet letters
- Scissors
- Sticker: three-dimensional hat
- Wire spiral clip: lavender

Directions

Trace Congrats Flap Card template (page 136) onto lavender cardstock; cut out. Score and fold flaps over. Cut one decorative paper to fit larger (left-side) flap, a second decorative paper to fit smaller (right-side) flap; glue both in place.

Stamp Congrats along top edge of left flap, and Reduate on right flap. Cut 2" square of white cardstock then adhere to 1³/₄" square of lavender cardstock. Apply sticker, add spiral clip, and mount to right flap of front of card.

Make a pocket for inside of card to tuck in a gift card, photo, movie tickets, etc. To make pocket, cut small rectangle out of third decorative paper. Apply small amount of adhesive to bottom of paper and adhere to inside of card; secure sides with brads.

Wine
Tasting
Tour

Chapter 4

We Gather Just Because!

There may be no rhyme or reason
We wait for no date or no season
We gather together, in all sorts of weather
For silliness, fun, and teasin'.

Decked in our velvets and leathers
And wrapped in long boas of feathers
We're out party-hopping or in the mall shopping
We've all gotten loose from our tethers.

Together we always have fun
Sometimes in the rain, sometimes in the sun
There'll always be plenty of time for those chores
We'd rather be out with those friends we adore.

—Ruby RedHat

Wine Tasting Invite

Materials

- ½" button: metal
- Acid-free adhesive
- Brads: square, 4
- Cardstock: natural
- Decorative paper: green harlequin, purple harlequin
- Fibers: green, purple
- Fine-point felt-tip pen: black
- Inkpads: green, purple
- Pencil
- Rubber stamps: grapes, leaves
- Scissors
- Sponge
- Tag template
- Wire spiral clip

Directions

Cut and fold cardstock into 5½" x 4¼" top-fold card. Cut purple harlequin to 3" x 4"; adhere to left side of card. Cut green harlequin to 2⅛" x 4"; adhere to right side of card.

Trace tag template on cardstock; cut out. Decorate with rubber stamps then sponge edges of tag with purple ink. Adhere tag to front of card at slight angle. Adhere metal button to right of tag then tie on purple and green fibers. Set brads in corners of card. Cut 2" x 1½" piece of cardstock; apply purple ink with sponge. Cut 1½" x 1¼" piece of cardstock; write Wine Tasting Tour with black pen. Layer cardstock then adhere to front of card.

Invite your friends to a wine tasting they'll savor long after the party. Many wines are red, so it's a perfect reason for a gathering—as if we need one!

Let's Play Card

Materials

- Acid-free adhesive
- Cardstock: red
- Decorative paper: red striped
- Embroidery needle
- Fine-point felt-tip pen: black
- Inkpad: red
- Rubber stamps: alphabet letters, stars
- Scissors
- Vellum tags: small, 3
- Waxy flax: red

Directions

Cut and fold cardstock into 3" x 3" top-fold card. Stamp stars randomly on front of card and once on each tag; let dry.

Adhere small strip of decorative paper across top of card. Stamp words Let's Play on bottom of card. Outline letters with black pen.

Poke hole through top of each tag with embroidery needle then string red waxy flax through tags and around card front; tie in double knot at front.

I still remember how polite we used to be about calling our childhood friends to see if they could play. Today we don't need permission from anyone, but we can still ask nicely!

Water Bottle Wrapper

Materials

- ¼" ribbon: lavender
- Cardstock: white
- Hook-and-loop tape
- Inkpads: lavender, purple, red
- Laminating machine and contact paper
- Rubber stamps: designs of your choice
- Scissors
- Water bottle

Directions

Cut strip of cardstock to fit bottle with some overlap. Stamp label for bottle. Laminate using clear contact paper. Attach wrapper to water bottle with hook-and-loop tape at back (this will allow you to remove and reuse wrapper with ease). Tie ribbon around neck of water bottle.

While I chose dots, stars, and hearts, you could stamp names on your wrappers to prevent mixing up bottles.

Poultry Idea

The Scarlet O'Hatters from the Prairie (Vandalia, Missouri) celebrated their chapter's first anniversary with a pajama breakfast. In addition to prizes for the best PJ outfit, best breakfast hat, and best house slippers, a rather ingenious recognition was initiated. The Chicken Award was given to the Red Hatter who failed to look as silly as the rest of her chapter. The award is now given at events as necessary.

Mini Table Bag

Materials

- ⅛" ribbon: purple
- Acid-free adhesive
- Decorative paper: red and purple floral
- Gift bag: mini pink
- Scissors
- Sticker: embossed words
- Tag template

Directions

Trace tag template on decorative paper; cut out. Adhere ribbon to front of bag. Add sticker to front of tag then adhere tag on top of ribbon on bag. Fill with goodies (sweets are always good) and place on table.

Table favors are always appreciated, especially when they contain my favorite food group—chocolate!

Nothing to Wine About

Some Red Hatters take their dress code very seriously. Members of the Rubies With HATtitude (Morris County, New Jersey), dressed in purple T-shirts and red hats, hiked up their skirts and jumped in a barrel for some good old-fashioned grape stomping at a local winery. By the time they finished, the color of their feet matched their shirts.

Movie Night Popcorn Invite

Materials

- Acid-free adhesive
- Brads: red, 2
- Cardstock: purple, red
- Decorative paper: paper of your choice
- Embroidery needle
- Fine-point felt-tip pen: black
- Inkpads: black, purple, red, yellow
- Microwave popcorn
- Pencil
- Rickrack: red
- Rubber stamp: popcorn bowl
- Scissors
- Tag template
- Vellum tag
- Water brush
- Waxy flax: lavender, red
- Wire spiral clip: red

Directions

Cut strip of purple cardstock and decorative paper to fit around popcorn with some overlap. Wrap around popcorn and adhere at back. Tie rickrack around popcorn. Trace tag onto red cardstock then cut out. Trace smaller tag on decorative paper; cut out then adhere to larger tag. Stamp popcorn bowl on vellum tag using black ink. Color in popcorn bowl with water brush. Poke hole at top of vellum tag using embroidery needle. Tie vellum tag onto larger tag using two colors of waxy flax. Add brads and wire spiral clip to bottom of tag. Tie tag to rickrack with waxy flax.

Write the details of the day on a decorative tag tied onto your Movie Night Popcorn Invite.

Shop 'Til You Drop Tag

Materials

- ½" ribbon: sheer white
- Acid-free adhesive
- Beaded wire
- Cardstock: natural, purple, white
- Decorative paper: red striped
- Eyelet setting tools
- Eyelets: purple, 2
- Hole punch
- Inkpads: black, purple, red
- Mulberry paper: purple
- Pencil
- Rubber stamps: gift bags, Shop 'Til You Drop
- Scissors
- Sponge
- Water brush

Directions

To make card: Cut white cardstock to 4¼" x 9". Score card 3½" from bottom edge. Fold up. Glue decorative paper on front pieces. Attach mulberry paper to inside of folded piece. Attach eyelets to top of folded piece. String ribbon through, tying off and finishing with bow. Cut purple cardstock to 4¾" x 2¼". Layer with slightly smaller piece of natural cardstock. Stamp natural cardstock with gift bag images, coloring in with purple and red ink. Attach cardstock to front of folded piece.

To make bookmark: Draw bookmark onto natural cardstock; cut out. Stamp Shop 'Til You Drop image on front; color in with water brush. Hole punch top of bookmark then string through beaded wire. With sponge and black ink, wipe edges and around hole punch of bookmark.

A folded card on the bag front is the perfect place to tuck in your bookmark.

Shopping Bag Card

Materials

- ½" ribbon: sheer white
- Acid-free adhesive
- Cardstock: purple, red
- Decorative paper: red and white striped
- Fine-point felt-tip pens: black, red
- Inkpads: purple, red
- Rubber stamps: gift bags
- Scissors
- Water brush

Directions

Cut and fold red cardstock into 6" x 6" side-fold card. Cut 5" square in middle of front of card by making large X then cutting on X; tear the triangle pieces.

Adhere 5" square piece of decorative paper to inside of card. Cut purple cardstock to 3" square; cut red cardstock to 2¾" square; cut white cardstock to 2½" square then layer the three cardstocks.

Stamp white cardstock with shopping bag images then color in with water brush, alternating purple and red ink. Attach ribbon in bottom right corner.

Usually there is one chapterette who has done lots of work organizing an outing. Show her your appreciation by sending a card with your thanks. You may even convince her to take charge of the next spree.

Spa Day Bath Salts & Tag

Materials

- ½" ribbon: red
- Acid-free adhesive
- Bath salts
- Cardstock: purple, white
- Feather: red
- Glass bottle
- Hole punch
- Inkpad: purple
- Pencil
- Scissors
- Stickers: alphabet letters
- Tag template

Directions

Fill glass bottle with bath salts; set aside. Trace tag template onto purple cardstock; cut out. Trace slightly smaller tag onto white cardstock; cut out then adhere to purple tag. Add alphabet stickers to front of white tag. Hole punch tag then tie tag and feather to glass bottle with ribbon.

A long soak can do wonders to revive the body after a happy outing. A gift of bath salts, wrapped in Red Hat style, is sure to encourage a friend to take soak time for herself.

Café au Red Hatters

Ever since the Red Bonnets & Bifocals (Butler, Pennsylvania) have been meeting for coffee on Tuesdays twice a month, the café manager has stopped by to say hello and tell them how much she enjoys seeing the group. To honor her favorite customers, the manager requested that all of her employees wear purple on Tuesdays, in honor of the Red Bonnets & Bifocals. From T-shirts to ruffled blouses, employees now don purple or lavender shirts.

Pajama Party Candle Tag

Materials

- 1/8" ribbon: purple sheer
- Acid-free adhesive
- Candle
- Decorative-edge scissors
- Decorative paper: coordinating patterns, 2
- Glue dot
- Scissors

Directions

Cut strip of decorative paper to fit around candle with some overlap. Cut second band slightly smaller with decorative-edge scissors. Layer both bands then adhere at back of candle with glue dot. Tie ribbon around candle.

Ballad for the Bride

The Ladies of Note (Ballston Lake, New York) gathered to celebrate the impending nuptials of a fellow Red Hatter's daughter. They met for brunch and launched the wedding festivities by serenading the bride with The Irish Blessing. She modeled her wedding gown, complete with a red boa (for the day), and the ladies presented her with a basket festooned with red and purple ribbons and filled with kitchen items and little anecdotes about some of their fun-filled outings.

Take-home gifts are as fun to give as to receive. A decorated candle makes a perfect party favor.

Tea Invite, Menu, Place Card & Favor Basket

Materials

- ¼" ribbon: sheer purple
- Acid-free adhesive
- Cardstock: white
- Computer and printer
- Decorative paper: purple polka dot, red and pink striped
- Die cuts: daisies, 10
- Eyelet setting tools
- Eyelets: purple, 8
- Favor box
- Fine-point felt-tip pen: black
- Foam square
- Hole punch: small
- Inkpad: purple
- Pencil
- Scissors
- Sequins: pink
- Vellum envelope: square

Directions

Print invitation, menu, and name tag information on computer printer. Cut to desired sizes.

To make menu and invite: Cut white cardstock to desired sizes. Add red and pink striped paper to cover front of cardstock. Add piece of purple polka dot paper to front. Add cardstock with tea details to front; set purple eyelet in each corner then embellish with daisy die cuts. *Note:* Invite should be about ⅛" smaller than vellum envelope.

To make place card: Cut and fold white cardstock in half to 3" x 1½". Adhere purple polka dot paper to place card. Cut name tag to 2½" x ¾"; adhere to place card. Add name and detailing around edge with black pen. Add two die-cut daisies; embellish centers with pink sequins.

To make favor basket: Adhere red and pink striped paper to base of favor box. Adhere strips of purple polka dot paper to sides of basket and handles. Embellish with daisy die cuts, adhering one of flowers with foam square. Cut tag out of white cardstock; embellish with die cut and decorative paper then punch hole at top. Tie tag to handle with purple ribbon.

MENU
Tarragon Chicken Tea Sandwiches
Minted Melon Salad
Sweet Honey Anise Biscuits
Peppermint Shortbread
Streusel Teacake
Chocolate Dipped Shortbread

Ruby

Ruby

An Afternoon Tea

Date: The 11th day of June

Time: 2:00 in the afternoon

Place: Rose Tea Garden

(555) 641-2222

Chapter 5

We Have a Happy Hattitude!

You can choose to live life in a glum or glad way
To be whiny and crabby or joyful and gay.

Smile just because there is good in this life
Or grumble and whine, concentrate on the strife.

Clap a hat on your head and go out and be bold
Or sit in the house by yourself and grow old.

Each one of us chooses her own view of things
We sit down and mope, or we choose to have wings.

So gather with friends who are friendly and merry
And top off the sundae of life with a cherry!
—Ruby RedHat

Hat Box Tag

Materials

- Acid-free adhesive
- Cardstock: purple, red, white
- Eyelet setting tools
- Eyelet: red
- Inkpad: lavender
- Pencil
- Ribbon
- Scissors
- Sponge
- Stickers: hat, flowers
- Tag template
- Water brush
- Wire spiral clip: lavender

Directions

Trace tag template on purple cardstock. Trace tag template on red cardstock slightly smaller; cut out then layer on purple tag. Trace smaller third layer of tag on white cardstock; cut out.

Wipe lavender ink around edge of white cardstock tag with sponge; dot ink with tip of water brush then dot all over white tag. Adhere this final tag to top.

Embellish tag with stickers, spiral clip, or whatever else you desire. Set eyelet at top of tag; thread through ribbon and tie in knot.

Tagging a box with the name of the contents makes it easy to find whatever part of your regalia you need.

Tag Bracelet

Materials

- Beads: assorted purple, red, and silver
- Fine-point felt-tip pen: black
- Heat embossing tool
- Hole punch
- Inkpads: purple, red
- Jewelry elastic
- Jump rings
- Rubber stamp: small flower
- Sandpaper
- Scissors
- Shrink plastic

Directions

Sand shrink plastic lightly with sandpaper. (This helps to hold ink better.) Stamp flowers in middle of tags, alternating purple and red ink.

Cut into tag shapes. Outline edge with pen. Punch hole at top before shrinking. Hole will shrink too, so use regular size hole punch. Heat either in oven as directions indicate on shrink paper or with heat embossing tool. To make bracelet, string jewelry elastic with beads of choice. Add tags to jump rings then attach to bracelet.

The tags on this bracelet are made by decorating shrink plastic and then heating them to size. Do you suppose it would work on Red Hatters who could be made into my own size?

Red Hatters Matter Lapel Pin

Materials

- Acid-free adhesive
- Cardboard circle
- Glitter: red
- Glitter glue
- Pin back
- Sticker

Directions

Attach sticker of your choice to cardboard circle. Line circle edges with glitter glue then sprinkle on glitter. Attach pin back with adhesive. Here we tied a purple ribbon around the vase then attached the lapel pin.

When you make your own jewelry, you are sure to be an original. This lapel pin says it all—Red Hatters do matter!

A Changed Life

The Queen Mother of the Razzle Dazzle Chix (Grafton, Wisconsin) changed her life as a widow when she joined the Red Hat Society. Rather than working and occasional dinners out, her days are now fun-filled with fashion shows, luncheons, tours, shopping, and senior exercise classes. And best of all, she says, her children are thrilled at her new hattitude!

Scrapbook Card

Materials

- Acid-free adhesive
- Cardstock: purple, white
- Decorative paper: coordinating patterns, 2
- Inkpad: purple
- Lapel pin
- Rubber stamp: your choice of small stamp
- Scissors

Directions

Cut and fold white cardstock into 6" x 6" top-fold card. Cut two 3" squares from two different decorative papers. Cut squares into triangles and arrange as shown in project. Adhere in place.

Cut purple cardstock to 4½" x 2½"; adhere to front of card. Cut white cardstock to 4" x 2". Adhere on top of purple cardstock. Decorate with stamp of your choice in each corner. Attach lapel pin to card front.

A thoughtful way to add a little gift to a card is to attach a lapel pin to the front. A pair of earrings would work well too. Diamonds or pearls would be nice, don't you think?

Hat Tag

Materials

- Acid-free adhesive
- Cardstock: white
- Decorative paper: red swirls
- Fine-point felt-tip pen: black
- Hole punch
- Pencil
- Ribbon or embroidery floss
- Rubber stamps: alphabet letters
- Scissors
- Sticker: hat
- Tag template

Directions

Trace tag template on cardstock; cut out. Embellish with decorative paper, stamped images, hand lettering, or stickers. Hole punch top of tag. Tie embroidery floss or ribbon through hole.

Rather than wear my feelings on my sleeve, I wear them on the brim of my hat. Hat tags can easily be changed with my mood.

A Bra-HaHa's Stirring

Laughter is the best medicine, and some Red Hatters are more than happy to deliver some belly-aching humor. Every year the Red Hat Mommas of Western Maine (Rumford, Maine) participate in a local hospital's health program for women as part of National Women's Health Week. One year, to raise the participants' spirits, the chapter's Vice Queen arrived with her red bra hat and matching purse. She was greeted by a room of giggling women who admired her creative attire and caught her infectious Red Hat Society spirit.

Savvy Shopper Bag & Tag

Materials

- ⅛" ribbon: red
- Acid-free adhesive
- Cardstock: purple, red, white
- Curly ribbon: assorted colors
- Embroidered patch: Ruby RedHat (optional)
- Embroidery thread: purple
- Fine-point felt-tip pen: black
- Gift bag: lavender
- Hole punch
- Pencil
- Rubber stamp: small gift bag
- Scissors
- Tag template: small
- Tissue paper: purple

Directions

To make tag: Trace tag template on white cardstock; cut out. Outline edge of tag with black pen and write Savvy Shopper at top of tag.

Add layer of purple cardstock to bottom half of tag; trim edges. Stamp white cardstock with gift bag image and embellish; cut out. Attach gift bag to red ribbon with embroidery thread, then add ribbon and embroidery thread at middle of tag.

Tie tag to gift bag handle with embroidery thread. Add embroidered patch of Ruby RedHat to bag or any other sticker of choice. Insert tissue paper.

I insist on being savvy—it keeps me on the cutting edge. To keep things fun and silly, to the Red Hatters I did pledge. It is with this sincere intention that this project draws attention.

Tag Booklet

Materials

- Acid-free adhesive
- Assorted embellishments
- Cardstock: white
- Decorative paper: 5-6 coordinating patterns
- Eyelet setting tools
- Eyelets
- Hole punch
- Pencil
- Ribbons
- Scissors

Directions

Trace Tag Booklet template (page 137) on cardstock; cut out. Score and fold between tags.

Embellish as desired with decorative papers, buttons, stickers, stamps, wire clips, rhinestones, brads, and any other details or photos your heart desires.

You may also want to punch holes or add eyelets at the top of the pointed tags then attach ribbons.

To help you get the perfect fold, consider using a bone folder on the fold lines of the Tag Booklet.

Friends Tag

Materials

- Acid-free adhesive
- Cardstock: purple, red
- Decorative paper: floral, purple harlequin, red plaid
- Eyelet: purple
- Eyelet setting tools
- Pencil
- Ribbon or tulle: purple
- Scissors
- Sequins: red
- Sticker: border, Friends
- Tag template

Directions

Trace tag template on purple cardstock; cut out. Cover $^2/_3$ of tag with decorative paper; layer strip of red plaid paper then add border sticker on top. Adhere row of sequins at top of plaid paper then add Friends sticker at bottom of tag. Add $^1/_2$" square piece of red cardstock to top center of tag; set eyelet in middle. Finish with purple ribbon or tulle tied through eyelet at top of tag.

I love the look of tulle for the bow, but you may choose a ribbon instead. As long as it's red or purple, anything goes.

Bookmark Holder

Materials

- Acid-free adhesive
- Bookmark
- Cardstock: purple
- Decorative paper: red and purple floral, small striped
- Eyelet setting tools
- Eyelets: purple, 4
- Scissors
- Sticker: hat
- Vellum paper

Directions

Cut cardstock to 3 1/2" x 8". Layer with red and purple floral paper 3 1/4" x 7 3/4" in center of cardstock.

Cut thin strip of small striped paper and attach to top edge of 3 1/2" vellum square.

Make pocket by attaching 3 1/2" square of vellum to bottom of project using eyelets in all four corners.

Add sticker to bottom of vellum. Insert bookmark in pocket.

When we're not being silly, some of us actually read! Present a Red Hat Society bookmark with a decorative bookmark holder.

There is no such thing as too much SPARKLE

I dream in COLOR

7♣

forever young

Chapter 6

We are Such Cards!

We use trading cards in our "business" of fun
We can make them en masse; we can make only one.

We adorn them with glitter, with sparkle and paint
We create tiny wonders of art sans restraint.

Each little card tells the world who I am
What I like, where I live. You can see, I'm a ham.

I keep my friends' cards in a fun little book
It's great to sit down and just take a look.

Recalling the sisters I've met near and far
Helps in keeping my memory far above par.

Remembering where I had fun with each one
A record of so many friendships begun!
　　　　　　　　　　—Ruby RedHat

Playing Card

Materials

- Acid-free adhesive
- Acrylic paints: purple, red
- Beaded trim
- Beads: assorted
- Feather trim
- Fine-point felt-tip pen: black
- Mulberry paper: pink
- Photograph
- Playing card
- Scissors

Directions

With finger and acrylic paints, create swirly design on playing card. Add torn strips of mulberry paper on tag; write note with black pen. Cut or tear photograph of your favorite Red Hatter and position on card. Add trims, beads, glitter, or whatever you desire to decorate.

I let my cards be an expression of my favorite sayings or mottos for life and embellish them with paint, paper, and beaded and feather trim.

A Rose in Bloom

The motto of the Perennials Chapter (Lafayette, Indiana) is, "We bloom every year!" So you can imagine the delight of a Red Hatter at a bridal shower held in her honor, where she was roasted and toasted with champagne and bubbles and presented with a red garter with purple ribbon, a red bridal veil, white slippers with red hearts, and a crystal serving bowl in the shape of a hat with red and purple stripes. It certainly was the ideal occasion for this red rose to bloom.

Box Top Card

Materials

- Acid-free adhesive
- Lace: red
- Mulberry paper: red
- Picture
- Playing card
- Rub-on letters
- Sticker: Ruby RedHat

Directions

Tear mulberry paper slightly larger than playing card; adhere to top of box. Decorate playing card with lace, sticker, picture, and rub-on word Imagine two times. Adhere card to mulberry paper on box.

This very simple project is ideal for decorating the top of a wooden box freshly painted in a delightful shade of purple—or you may prefer red.

Didn't Your Mother Ever Tell You...

While out to lunch with her chapterettes, a member of the Rhinestones chapter (Chula Vista, California) was approached at the buffet table by a well-dressed woman. She leaned over and said, "Didn't your mother ever tell you not to wear purple and red together?" The queen mother pointed to her table of 15 Red Hatters and said, "Oh really? I guess you better tell them too." Her mouth fell open as she looked in dismay at all of the women dressed in bright red and purple.

Trading Card Holder

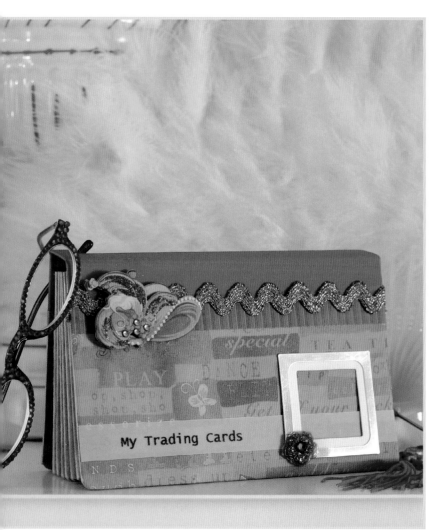

Materials

- Accordion file folder: small
- Acid-free adhesive
- Computer and printer
- Decorative paper: coordinating patterns, 2
- Rickrack: purple
- Scissors
- Scrapbook frame
- Sticker: red hat, raised purple flower
- Vellum paper

Directions

Note: We were lucky when we came across this file folder with a red spine. If your folder is not bedecked in this radiant color, paint spine or adhere red cardstock.

Cut and adhere both coordinating decorative paper to bottom $^2/_3$ of front of file folder. Add rickrack, stickers, and scrapbook frame. We also printed out My Trading Cards on vellum using a computer and printer and adhered it to the front. Fill with your favorite Red Hatter cards!

While this holder is ideal for trading cards, you could also use it to hold coupons or recipes.

Decorated Playing Cards

Materials

- Acid-free adhesive or decoupage medium
- Buttons
- Cardstock: purple, red
- Decorative paper: coordinating patterns
- Doily
- Inkpad: brown
- Mulberry paper: natural, red
- Playing card
- Scissors
- Sponge
- Stickers: various embossed, alphabet letters
- Trims

Directions

Using playing card as template, trace onto both red and purple cardstock; cut out. To create "aged" look, rub on light application of brown ink with sponge. Embellish to your heart's contents with odds and ends like buttons, trim, decorative paper, stickers, and paper doily. Adhere items with decoupage medium or adhesive.

Clip your cards just about anywhere with tiny wooden clothespins in fun colors. They'll have to be small—like me!

Business Card Necklace

Materials

- Acid-free adhesive
- Beads: 3
- Cardstock: lavender
- Cord: red

- Decorative paper
- Fibers
- Hole punch
- Hook-and-loop dot

- Inkpad: purple
- Rubber stamp: flower
- Scissors
- Water brush (optional)

Directions

Trace Business Card Necklace template (page 137) on cardstock; cut and score on fold lines. Punch two holes in each side as indicated; fold on all score lines. Stamp flower image all over cardstock. Place adhesive on two long outside flaps (marked "A"). Fold up box so both "A" flaps are glued to edges marked "B." Let dry.

Slip cord through holes in one side of box so a few inches of cord are hanging out of bottom hole. Place three beads on cord and tie knot just above beads. Adjust length of cord as needed, then repeat on other side of box.

Place "hook" dot on inside of top flap and "loop" dot on front of box so hook and loop will match up when closed. Decorate front as desired with paper, stickers, or rubber stamps.

A hook-and-loop dot makes opening and closing your Business Card Necklace a cinch.

Tag Card

Materials

- Acid-free adhesive
- Cardstock: white
- Decorative papers: coordinating patterns, 2
- Glitter
- Inkpad
- Rubber stamps
- Scissors
- Stickers: concho, 3
- Wire spiral clip: white

Directions

Cut cardstock to 4" x 5 ½"; round off corners. Decorate as desired with decorative paper, rubber stamps, concho stickers, and spiral clip.

Wire clips come in silver and gold, and a host of other colors. They are fine embellishments to cards and tags.

A Red and Purple Thumb

They say one woman's junk is another woman's treasure. So leave it up to a Red Hatter to turn that treasure into a garden delight! A member of the Fabulous Foxy Fedoras (Grand Island, Nebraska) painted her old claw-foot tub purple, and then planted it with red geraniums and purple carnations. A white trellis was added at the back, and its crowning touch? A red hat, of course!

It's All About Me Card

Materials

- ½" buttons: red, 2
- Acid-free adhesive
- Cardstock: white
- Decorative paper: purple harlequin, red floral
- Rub-on letters
- Scissors
- Scrapbook frame: small

Directions

Cut cardstock to 4" x 5½". Layer with decorative paper; tear edge at angle for added interest. Embellish with buttons and small scrapbook frame. Add wording It's All About with rub-on letters at top of card. Add square piece of white cardstock at center of card. Complete card by adding photograph.

Just as the Tag Card reads, be sure to place your favorite photo in the center square.

'Red Alert' Support

When the Red Hat Hottentots (North Olmstead, Ohio) first got together, Queen Buttercream (a cake decorator by profession) listed a handful of courtesies bestowed on her fellow chapterettes. In the spirit of sisterhood, No. 6 reads: "A Red Hat should always come to the aid of another—and pass the word on—so we all stand united wherever we're needed." This will be known as the "Red Alert" and those who can are expected to be on the scene ASAP to lend support.

Chapter 7

Red Hatters Always Shine!

The Queen has declared that gaudy is good
She loves things that sparkle, we knew she would.

Sprinkles of twinkles and refracted light
Make Red-Hatted sisters a dazzling sight.

The bigger the sparkle, the better the shine
The glitziest, ritziest that we can find.

Maybe some diamonds, perhaps dime-store glitter
The bolder it is, the more that we titter.

Some say that a diamond is a woman's best friend
But with our faux jewels we're starting a trend!

—Ruby RedHat

Candy Bag Topper

Materials

- Acid–free adhesive
- Brads: red, 6
- Candy
- Cardstock: purple, white
- Cellophane bag
- Inkpad: purple
- Rubber stamps: alphabet letters
- Scissors
- Scrapbook frame: large
- Stapler

Directions

Cut and fold cardstock into 4¼" x 3" top-fold card. Stamp For You! on square piece of white cardstock using purple ink.

Layer white square onto folded cardstock. Attach large frame over words. Attach three sets of brads on each side of frame. Fill bag with candy. Secure bag topper to top of bag with stapler.

This candy bag ensemble is so easy to make—and it looks like it came right off the shelf of a candy store.

Thinking Outside the Box

Remember the "olden days," when there were box lunch affairs? Women brought a box lunch in a pretty container and men bid on the lunch. The Decatur Red Hot Red Hat Readers (Decatur, Tennessee) held its own box luncheon, where each chapterette packed a lunch of her own making, plain or fancy, and brought it in a decorated box. As the ladies arrived, their box was given a number. When everyone was seated, a cup of corresponding numbers was passed around. Each lady drew a number and got a lunch of delicious proportions.

Layered Napkin Ring

Materials

- Decorative paper: coordinating patterns, 3
- Glue dots
- Ruler
- Scissors

Directions

Cut red paper to 3½" x 5"; secure at back with glue dot. Cut second coordinating paper to 2" x 5"; secure at back with glue dot. Cut third strip of coordinating paper about ½" x 5"; secure at back with glue dot. Snip edges of largest paper (in our case the red paper) every ⅛" with scissors, taking care to not cut layered band; fold up ends of tiny strips with fingers.

I couldn't find the right napkin ring so I made my own by layering different red and purple papers.

An Indelible Impression

When one of the princesses of the Red Hat Rolling Stones (Lone Rock, Wisconsin) reached her 50th birthday, she celebrated with a reduation to be remembered. In honor of the occasion, fellow chapterettes gave her a party, of course, but then she and three other Red Hatters went "above and beyond" and got tattoos of red hats, designed by the honoree, Queen Morning Light.

Her Majesty Hat Tag

Materials

- Acid-free adhesive
- Cardstock: red
- Decorative paper
- Eyelet: gold
- Eyelet setting tools
- Fine-point felt-tip pen: black
- Glitter: purple
- Pencil
- Queen Mother lapel pin
- Red velvet paper
- Ribbon
- Scissors
- Sticker machine and permanent adhesive
- Tag template

Directions

Trace and cut tags, one smaller out of cardstock, one larger out of red velvet paper. Run cardstock tag through sticker machine. Peel off protective sheet. Apply glitter to sticky side of tag; let dry completely.

Layer glittered tag onto red velvet paper tag. Set gold eyelet using eyelet setting tools at top of tag. Layer red strip of velvet paper along bottom of tag and write Her Majesty with black pen. Attach Queen Mother lapel pin to front of tag. String through your ribbon of choice.

Left: I couldn't resist fanciful colors on this party table. To make the centerpiece, I inserted an empty water bottle in the center of a glass vase then lined rows of colored jelly beans between the water bottle and the vase and tucked in suckers. Curly ribbon makes the perfect finishing touch.

Right: Secure the lapel pin at the back of the tag.

Gad About Shaker Card

Materials

- Acid-free adhesive
- Cardstock: purple, white
- Foam strips
- Glitter: red and purple
- Metal scrapbooking details
- Rub-on alphabet letters
- Scissors
- Scrapbooking frames: large, 2
- Seed beads: purple, red
- Stickers: floral, Ruby RedHat

Fill card with glitter, charms, favorite stickers, or just about anything else that comes in red and purple.

Directions

Cut white cardstock to fit between frames; add sticker. Layer frames with white cardstock in between; secure with adhesive on three sides.

Cut and fold purple cardstock into 5" x 7" side-fold card. Fill inside of frame with seed beads, sticker, metal scrapbooking details, and glitter.

Adhere to front of card with foam strips. Embellish frame with stickers. Apply Gad About alphabet letters on top of frame.

Christmas in July

Undeterred by a 115-degree heat wave, members of the Crimson Royalty of Shawnee chapter (Shawnee, Kansas) enjoyed their Christmas in July with a gift and cookie exchange. They lunched and munched, gleefully sharing some wonderful recipes. One Red Hatter, battling the heat yet determined to participate, made chocolate "no bake" cookies to share. Now that's a cool idea!

Giggle Card

Materials

- Acid-free adhesive
- Brads: silver, 2
- Cardstock: purple
- Glitter: purple
- Glitter glue
- Inkpads: purple, red
- Rubber stamp: small daisy
- Scissors
- Vellum tag
- Velvet paper: red

Directions

Cut and fold cardstock into 3" x 3" top-fold card. Stamp daisy on cardstock using purple ink. Stamp daisy on velvet paper using red ink. Layer red paper on purple card.

Write word Giggle and draw daisies on vellum tag with glitter glue. Sprinkle on purple glitter; tap off excess and let dry. Attach tag to front of card using silver brads.

Remind your fellow Red Hatters to take time to giggle at your next hattering with a Giggle Card.

Living it up in NYC

One year, the Bernadette Busy Buddies (St. Louis, Missouri) took a trip to New York City. Arriving in Red Hat style, chapterettes stepped out of their limo and into a world of shopping, sightseeing, and glamorous nights out. It was a week of fun and frivolity, and they enjoyed great laughs painting the town red and purple.

Paper Purse

Materials

- Acid-free adhesive
- Boa: red
- Buttons: 2
- Cardstock: white
- Decorative paper: coordinating patterns, 2
- Decorative-edge scissors
- Pencil
- Scissors
- Sticker: hat

Directions

Trace Paper Purse templates (page 136) and copy on cardstock two times (you will have one extra flap piece and one extra base piece; discard). Cut out pieces then adhere decorative paper to each piece.

To assemble purse: Fold purse base at the bottom and at right and left as shown on template. By folding up about ½" of each end, attach shortest strips of template to sides, medium length to bottom, and largest strip will serve as handle at top of purse.

Add hat sticker to folded-over flap. Adhere boa to handle and button on each side where handle stops.

I love to fill these paper purses with candy treats. They are pretty on the table and fun take-home gifts.

Elan Card

Materials

- Acid-free adhesive
- Cardstock: purple, white
- Inkpad: purple
- Rubber stamps: alphabet letters
- Sponge brayer
- Sticker: large red hat
- Stripe template

Directions

Cut and fold white cardstock into $5^{1}/_{2}$" x $4^{1}/_{4}$" top-fold card. Lay stripe template over front of card. Roll sponge brayer over ink, then roll over stripe stencil. Remove stencil when all areas have been covered.

Stamp words Elan along $5^{1}/_{2}$" x $1^{1}/_{2}$" strip of white cardstock. Layer on $5^{1}/_{2}$" x 2" strip of purple cardstock; adhere both to front of card. Add large hat sticker.

I made the stripes on the Elan Card myself and you can too. All you need is a stripe stencil available at most craft stores.

DIVA Tag

Materials

- ¹/₂" ribbon: lavender
- Acid-free adhesive
- Acrylic paint: purple
- Cardstock: purple
- Decorative paper: coordinating patterns, 3
- Die-cut letters: D, I, V, A
- Glitter: purple
- Glitter glue
- Hole punch
- Paintbrush
- Pencil
- Scissors
- Tag template

Directions

Paint letters with purple paint and sprinkle with glitter; set aside to dry. Trace tag template on purple cardstock; cut out. Layer decorative paper on front of tag. Adhere letters. Punch hole at top and tie ribbon.

Letters are available in die-cut and wooden forms. Both will do!

Yes I Can-Can!

Members of the Red Roses Chapter (Woodburn, Oregon) are kicking up their heels, entertaining audiences throughout their community with a show-stopping chorus line. Just goes to show that you can-can do anything you put your mind to!

Sequin Hat Card

Materials

- ⅛" sheer ribbon: purple
- Acid-free adhesive
- Cardstock: white
- Decorative paper: coordinating patterns, 2
- Doily: heart shaped
- Fabric sequin hat: red
- Ribbon
- Scissors

Directions

Cut and fold cardstock to 6" x 6" top-fold card. Cut and adhere your choice of decorative paper to cover front of card. Layer with smaller square of coordinating paper.

Adhere hat to doily; adhere doily to center of card. Attach ribbon at fold and tie into bow at top of card.

If your hat emblem doesn't have sequins—add them! I've always said, the more sparkle the better.

Survival Gear

When it comes to fun, The Reading Pagoda Chapter of the Red Hat Society (Reading, Pennsylvania) loves to show its true colors. Ready to head down the Delaware River on rafts, these Red Hatters insisted on red paddles. Luckily the activity group had the paddles and also red and purple life vests on hand, or else there would surely have been a Red Hatter revolt!

Hat Cutout Card

Materials

- Acid-free adhesive
- Cardstock: red
- Decorative paper: coordinating patterns, 2
- Die-cut shapes: flowers
- Glitter
- Glue pen
- Pencil
- Ribbon
- Scissors

Directions

Trace Hat Cutout Card template (page 137) on cardstock; cut out. Cover card with decorative paper. Adhere second decorative paper and ribbon to front, creating hatband. Adhere cutout flowers to side of hatband; embellish with glitter.

While my hatband is paper, you may want to use all ribbons for your Hat Cutout Card.

Southern Hospitality at its Best

Before leaving for the Tall Clubs International convention in Charleston, South Carolina, a few members of the Long Tall Sallies (Sacramento, California) thought it would be a blast to connect with fellow Red Hatters while on their trip. They posted a message on the Queen Mother Board and were enthusiastically answered with a lunch invitation from the Geechee Red Hatters of Charleston. On a hot and humid Saturday in Charleston, nine tall Red Hatters from all over the country joined about 25 members of the Geechee gals.

Metal Tag Trio Card

Materials

- Acid-free adhesive
- Cardstock: red, white
- Craft wire
- Decorative paper: red with white polka dots
- Eyelet setting tools
- Eyelets: silver, 3
- Metal tags: 3
- Sandpaper
- Scissors

Directions

Cut and fold white cardstock into 4" x 4" top-fold card. Adhere 1½" strip of red with white polka dots paper along top of card.

Sand red cardstock then tear top edge. Adhere to bottom ⅔ of card, overlapping red with white polka dots paper. Trim any overage.

Set three eyelets evenly spaced along top of card. Punch three holes in center of card, about 1" directly below previously placed eyelets. Glue metal tags over three bottom holes.

Cut three pieces of craft wire. From backside of card front, push wire through each set of eyelet and poked holes (and through top of tag); twist to secure. Twist loose wire ends into spirals.

Metal tags with a loop at the top to string through craft wire work best for this card project.

Friends & Sisters Tag Card

Materials

- Acid-free adhesive
- Cardstock: white
- Charms: red hats, 2
- Decorative paper: purple and red striped
- Eyelet setting tools
- Eyelets: purple, 3
- Glue dots
- Paper tag: red
- Scissors
- Sticker: Friends & Sisters
- Tags: metal rimmed, small square, 2; medium rectangle, 1
- Waxy flax: red

Directions

Cut and fold cardstock into 3" x 3" top-fold card. Cover front of card with 3" square of decorative paper. Decorate front of red paper tag with Friends & Sisters sticker. Adhere hat charms to center of small square tags with glue dot. Set purple eyelets in all tags. Adhere tags to front of card with glue dots. Tie waxy flax around middle of card.

I love to use glue dots when adding charms, beads, or baubles. They are easy to apply and there's no sticky glue mess.

Queen of Jewels

Nancy Gorski, queen of the Jacaranda Jewels (Venice, Florida), held a luncheon for her court and had the time of her life. Nancy adopted a Victorian theme and set her home ablaze in purple and red—hand towels, candles, and flowers were among the color decorations. Prizes were given for the prettiest hat, most creative outfit, and best overall regalia.

Forever Young Frame

Materials

- 1" masking tape
- Acrylic paint: red
- Cardstock: purple, white
- Fabric frame

- Foam dots
- Glitter: red
- Inkpad: purple
- Paintbrush

- Rubber stamps: alphabet letters
- Scissors
- Spray adhesive
- Stickers: assorted red hats

Directions

Paint front, back, and sides of frame red. Let dry. Evenly space masking tape along front of frame, leaving ³/₄" exposed between each tape. Spray with adhesive then sprinkle glitter on sprayed areas. Let dry then remove masking tape.

Cut 1" squares out of purple cardstock. Layer with slightly smaller white cardstock squares. Stamp individual letters on each white square to spell out Forever Young.

Adhere squares to front of frame with foam dots. Embellish with assorted red hat stickers. Add your favorite photo.

While I used a fabric-covered frame, a plain wooden frame would work well too.

Glitter Gift Box Tag

Materials

- Acid-free adhesive
- Cardstock: purple, white
- Decorative paper: red checkered
- Decorative-edge scissors
- Glitter: red
- Glitter glue
- Inkpad: purple
- Rubber stamp: gift box
- Scissors

Directions

To make card: Cut and fold purple cardstock into 2³/₄" x 2³/₄" top-fold card. Cut 2" square of white cardstock with decorative-edge scissors; adhere to front of card.

Stamp gift box on white cardstock. Using glitter glue, outline select portion of gift tag and sprinkle on glitter.

To make envelope: Cut 3" x 12" piece of red checkered paper. Fold in half with patterned sides touching. Fold again in quarters. Fold left top corner down to make triangle. Fold second quarter to right up at 45-degree angle. Fold into envelope.

Decorative-edge scissors give this card a pretty finishing touch.

Flower Brads Tag

Materials

- Acid-free adhesive
- Brads: red, 5
- Cardstock: purple, red
- Foam squares
- Metal flowers: tiny, 5
- Scissors
- Sticker: medium red hat

Directions

Cut and fold red cardstock into 3" x 3" top-fold card. Cut purple cardstock to 2³⁄₄" square; adhere to front of card. Add brads and metal flowers along bottom of card. Add hat sticker at top.

I attached the Flower Brads Tag to a ribbon to dress up a plain white pitcher.

Dyeing for a Good Time

Finding the right outfit is not always an easy task. One Red Hatter found this to be true when her chapter, the Lakewalk Ladies (Deluth, Minnesota), decided to have a garden party with a vintage theme. This Red Hatter, in her search for a vintage purple dress, hit every store in town, including a consignment store. Tired but determined, she put on her red thinking cap and headed to the grocery store for some purple dye. Before long, a plain dress became a sight of purple perfection thanks to a little ingenuity—and that thinking woman's red hat.

Purse Card

Materials

- Button
- Cardstock: lavender, white
- Decorative paper
- Exacto knife
- Hook-and-loop circle
- Inkpad: red
- Ribbon
- Rubber stamps
- Scissors
- Sticker: metal tag
- Tag template: small
- Waxy flax: lavender

Directions

Trace Purse Card & Tags templates (page 139) onto desired paper and cut out. If you want to keep semicircular flap, use Exacto knife to cut all but straight edge of semicircle. You may also create flap using strip of paper. Stamp on paper if desired to create your own background.

Cut contrasting piece of paper for flap on purse. Add button. Adhere hook-and-loop circle to close flap of purse.

To create tag: Trace template on lavender cardstock; cut out. Create slightly smaller tag using white cardstock; adhere to larger tag, then layer with metal tag sticker.

Since I love to shop, a purse is a great way to invite friends to a day at the mall.

Metal Heart Card

Materials

- Acid-free adhesive
- Beads: assorted
- Cardstock: white
- Decorative paper: purple harlequin
- Glue dots
- Inkpad: purple
- Metal heart emblem
- Scissors
- Sponge brayer
- Stripe template
- Waxy flax: purple

Directions

Cut and fold cardstock into 5" x 7" side-fold card. Lay stripe template on top of front of card. Roll sponge brayer over inkpad; roll over stencil to cover entire front of card.

Cut purple harlequin paper to 5" x 6". Tear top and bottom of paper. Tear out square of striped paper; adhere to purple harlequin paper with adhesive.

Tie waxy flax around metal heart emblem. Thread beads on waxy flax; tie at ends. Adhere metal heart emblem onto striped square with glue dots.

Embellish your cards to your heart's desire—I did! I found the heart in the scrapbooking section of my favorite crafts store.

Cupcake Card

Materials

- Acid-free adhesive
- Cardstock: purple, white
- Computer and printer
- Decorative paper: purple patterned
- Eyelash yarn
- Foam square
- Scissors
- Sticker: cupcake
- Wire spiral clips: purple, 2

Directions

Cut and fold white cardstock into 4¼" x 5½" side-fold card. Cut and adhere decorative paper to fit front of card.

Cut purple cardstock to 3½" x 2½"; adhere to front of card. Using computer and printer, print out witty quote or message of choice on white cardstock. Cut white cardstock to 3¼" x 2¼"; adhere to center of purple cardstock. Add cupcake sticker to front of card with foam square.

Embellish with spiral clips, one at top and one at bottom. Tie eyelash yarn around fold of card.

This cupcake looks good enough to eat. I added a foam square to the back then adhered it to the card front for extra interest.

Seize the moment. Remember all those women on the Titanic who waved off the dessert cart.
- Erma Bombeck

Laugh, Create, Celebrate Tag Card

Materials

- Acid-free adhesive
- Buttons: assorted small lavender, 3
- Cardstock: lavender, pink
- Embroidery needle
- Fine-point felt-tip pen: black
- Glue dots
- Inkpad: purple
- Rubber stamp: small swirl
- Scissors
- Vellum tags: assorted small sizes
- Waxy flax: lavender

Directions

Cut and fold lavender cardstock into 3" x 3" side-fold card. Cut pink cardstock to 2¹⁄₂" square; adhere to front of card. Stamp swirls randomly on both layers of each card front.

Write words on tags using black pen. Poke hole through top of tag with embroidery needle.

Tie piece of waxy flax to each tag. Attach to front of card. Fold ends of waxy flax over top of card; secure inside card. Add buttons using glue dots to adhere.

Laugh, celebrate, and create—these are three words I live by. What are your favorite words?

Chapter 8

We are Royal Regalitarians!

We know in some countries there's only one Queen
But that has all changed, here we ALL reign supreme.

Your title is any old name you may choose
Just be sure that it fits you, like comfortable shoes.

Perhaps you will call yourself Queen of Denial
(Touch base with reality once in a while).

The Dame of Disorder keeps things here and there
And Lady of Upkeep keeps track of just where.

The lady with jewels is the Duchess of Glitz
The one who's confused? Why, she's Duchess of Ditz.

So, your crown's only made of aluminum foil?
Whatever your title, be sure that it's royal!

—Ruby RedHat

Her Royal Highness Tag

Materials

- Beads: assorted
- Charms: red hats
- Embossing ink
- Embossing powder: red
- Eyelet: purple
- Eyelet setting tools
- Feather trim: purple
- Glitter: purple
- Glitter glue
- Sticker: small crown
- Vellum tag: metal-rimmed rectangle
- Waxy flax: purple, red

Directions

Emboss words Her Royal Highness with red embossing ink and powder on tag. Add sticker. Outline tag with glitter glue. Sprinkle glitter over glue; let dry. Set eyelet then tie trim and waxy flax on tag. Tie beads and charms on ends of waxy flax.

This royal tag, tied with pretty ribbons, makes a fun napkin ring.

Sitting Pretty

A handful of zany River City Hatters (LaCrosse, Wisconsin) went on the road for fun in Red Hat Society proportions. They visited Amana Colonies in Iowa, a national historic monument of seven quaint villages and home of the state's largest rocker. The five Red Hatters climbed on the 670-pound, 11-foot-tall solid walnut rocker and had their photo taken, looking like a group of mischievous schoolgirls with sparkles in their eyes.

Princess Tag

Materials

- $\frac{1}{8}$" ribbon: purple, red
- Acid-free adhesive
- Brads: gold, 4
- Cardstock: purple
- Decorative paper: coordinating patterns, 2
- Hole punch
- Princess lapel pin
- Rickrack: purple
- Scissors
- Tag: metal-rimmed square

Directions

Cut cardstock to 3" x 6 $\frac{1}{4}$". Layer with 2 $\frac{3}{4}$" x 6" piece of decorative paper. Attach brad to each corner. Adhere second decorative paper to metal-rimmed square tag. Adhere tag to front of project. Attach lapel pin to middle of square. Adhere rickrack around tag; secure at back with adhesive. Hole punch top of tag then tie one 7 $\frac{1}{2}$" length of each ribbon.

A Hunk of Burning Love

When it comes to glitz, the Amethyst Roses (Rockwood, Michigan) have met their match. While some thought they were having hot flashes, others swooned to the singing Elvis, bedecked in his jeweled white pantsuit. He may have been a world-champion impersonator, but these women definitely felt their temperatures rising!

While I chose a star lapel pin you could choose any shape. Just make sure it is small enough to fit in the square tag.

Royal Journal

Materials

- Acid-free adhesive
- Brad: red
- Cardstock: purple, white
- Composition book
- Decorative paper: red floral
- Die-cuts: alphabet, border
- Inkpads: purple, red
- Pencil
- Rubber stamps: alphabet letters, Duchess, Empress, Princess, Queen
- Scissors
- Stickers: border, crowns, flowers, red hats
- Tag template

Since I had a difficult time keeping track of my social schedule I decided I needed an organize-her.

Directions

Randomly stamp royal-themed words on white cardstock, alternating purple and red ink. Rotate words in different directions. Stamp twice before re-inking to give lighter shade of ink to some words.

Adhere white cardstock onto front and back of composition book, letting paper go over edges of book. It's easier to trim off excess after paper is glued onto book than to try and cut it exact size.

Layer border sticker along bottom of white cardstock. Add decorative paper to spine of book. Adhere 2 1/2" strips of purple cardstock down front and back of book. Personalize purple cardstock with die cuts and stickers. Trace tag template on purple cardstock; cut out. Personalize tag with die cuts and stickers. Add brad to tag; attach tag to front of journal.

Queen for A Day Card

Materials

- ¼" grosgrain ribbon: red
- Acid-free adhesive
- Cardstock: red, white
- Decorative paper: purple harlequin, red striped
- Inkpad: purple
- Playing card
- Rubber stamps: alphabet letters
- Scissors

Directions

Cut and fold white cardstock into 6" x 6" side-fold card. Cut and adhere red striped paper to outside of card.

Cut purple harlequin paper to 4" square. Wrap ribbon around paper then layer onto front of card.

Stamp Queen for a Day on 1½" white cardstock square. Layer white square on 2" red cardstock square. Adhere word square and playing card onto front of card.

Our playing cards add festive flair to this Queen for A Day card. I'll have to say I look quite dashing!

In Highway Style

More than two dozen members of the Red Hattitudes (DeWitt, Michigan) traveled by limousine to the Gem Theatre in Detroit, Michigan to see "Menopause The Musical." They ate the whole way there and laughed the whole way back.

Princess Card

Materials

- $\frac{1}{8}$" ribbon: lavender
- Acid-free adhesive
- Cardstock: lavender, purple, white
- Decorative paper: coordinating patterns, 2
- Eyelet setting tools
- Eyelets: purple, 3
- Inkpads: gold, purple
- Rubber stamps: crown, Princess
- Scissors
- Sponge dauber
- Vellum paper

Directions

Cut and fold lavender cardstock into 6" x 6" side-fold card. Layer 5½" square of decorative paper on cardstock, then layer second 5" decorative paper on top of that.

Cut white cardstock to 2" square. Sponge white square with dauber using gold ink. Stamp crown on middle of square using purple ink. Layer white, purple, and lavender squares.

Set eyelet at top of small square. Tie ribbon through eyelet. Add square to front of card.

Cut 5" strip of vellum paper then adhere to front of card using two eyelets. Stamp Princess in center of strip with purple ink.

It's so easy to create an aged look without getting older. Simply sponge ink around the edges and voilá.

Happy Coronation Day Card

Materials

- Acid-free adhesive
- Appliqué: crown
- Beaded trim: red
- Cardstock: red
- Decorative paper: purple polka dot
- Fine-point felt-tip pen: black
- Metallic paper: gold
- Photograph
- Scissors

Directions

Cut and fold cardstock into 5" x 7" side-fold card. Adhere 4" x 4³/₄" piece of gold metallic paper to front of card. Adhere decorative paper along bottom ¹/₃ of card. Trim photograph closely around person then adhere to gold paper. Add crown to top of her head. Adhere beaded trim to front of card. Write Happy Coronation Day on trim.

This big hat makes a big statement—and recalls a fun-filled coronation.

Under Red Hat Cover

Our Lady of the High Seize, a member of the Ocean View Red Hat Beach Babes (Norfolk, Virginia), also is a member of the Navy Reserve. She often attends Red Hat Society outings wearing a red hat and—you guessed it—combat boots. When shopping for red hats, she's typically out of uniform and under red cover.

Queen Bee Hat Tag

Materials

- Acid-free adhesive
- Brads: gold, 2
- Cardstock: red
- Eyelet: gold
- Eyelet setting tools
- Inkpad: black
- Lapel pin: bee
- Metallic paper: gold
- Pencil
- Rubber stamps: alphabet letters
- Tag template

Directions

Trace tag template on red cardstock; cut out. Trace slightly smaller tag template on gold metallic paper; cut out then adhere to red tag. Set eyelet at top of tag (over both tags). Pin bee onto tag. Stamp or write Queen Bee on red strip of paper; adhere to bottom of tag using brads.

This tag was made after my own heart with gold metallic paper and gold brads.

Titles for Regaltarians

Red Hatters are not only fun, they can be very funny. The Plum Crazy Crimson Cuties (Phoenix, Arizona) had a blast coming up with royal titles, including Delicious Vice Queen, High Priestess of Hilarity; Bobbin Robin, the Marchioness of Music; BoopADoop, Doris the Dowager of DoNuttin'; Classy Lassy, the Contessa of Calligraphy; Dashing Damsel, the Governess of Gatherings; Dangerous, the Dancing Duchess of Delphina; Dazzling Dixie Doll, the Vicountess of Volunteers; Jolly JuneBug, the Hysterical Historian; Lady JollyFingers, the Regent of Reservations; Madame Butterfly Babe, the Sultana of Silliness; and Pink Passion, the Czarina of Craftiness.

Glitter Queen Hat Tag

Materials

- Acid-free adhesive
- Cardstock: purple
- Die-cut tag: white
- Eyelash yarn
- Glitter: red, silver
- Glue pen
- Hole punch
- Inkpad: black
- Pencil
- Rubber stamps: alphabet letters
- Scissors

Directions

Trace tag onto cardstock; cut out slightly larger. Adhere tag to cardstock; trim to size. Stamp words Glitter Queen on tag. Using glue pen, trace words then sprinkle on silver glitter. Repeat around edge of card with red glitter. Hole punch top then tie with yarn.

A Regal Retreat

Four friends from high school, all about to reach their "Fifty and Fabulous" milestone, celebrated their induction into the Red Hat Society with a weekend away. The inaugural meeting of the MHS Scarlettes (Glen Williams, Ontario, Canada) were named after their alma mater, Mimico High School. To honor their newfound regal status, the Queen Mother was crowned with a gold and burgundy tea cozy. To show their allegiance to the Queen, each of her loyal subjects then got on bended knee and kissed her garnet ring.

Tags aren't just for bags, silly! I love the idea of hat tags for every Red Hatter at the party.

My Royal Court of Friends Photo Book

Materials

- Acid-free adhesive
- Beads
- Cardstock
- Decorative paper: coordinating patterns, 5
- Fibers
- Glitter
- Mat board or cardboard
- Pencil
- Ribbon: assorted red, purple, and lavender, 4
- Tag
- Vellum paper
- Waxy flax

These photo books are perfect for celebrating friendships and the things you love about your best gal pals.

Directions

Note: This project can be done with any size cardstock as long as you start with a square. Fold square in half vertically. Open. Fold in half horizontally. Open. Turn square over. Fold in half diagonally. Open. With pencil, draw two corners on ends of diagonally folded line down to meet each other. The square will naturally flatten into the shape you need. Your "chain" of folded squares can be any length you desire, you just need at least three and you need an odd number. Think of your folded shapes as mouths. They need to feed each other! Put one folded mouth into another folded mouth. Keep going to form chain.

To create covers: Cover two pieces of 4½" square mat board with decorative paper, just like you are wrapping a gift. Glue ribbons to back cover. Glue on front cover. Decorate inside of book using decorative paper, photos, quotes, or whatever you desire.

Glossary

Red Hat Society Terms

Birthday Suits (no, not that kind): A Red Hatter gains special attention by wearing the Red Hat colors in reverse during her birthday month. She wears a red outfit with a purple hat. We call this tradition "au contraire" (French for "to the contrary"). Why do we do this? Because we feel like it, and because we can. We are always on the lookout for ways to make life fun.

Brim-Brushing: Red Hatters enjoy gestures of affection when bidding each other hello or good-bye, but hugs tend to knock hats to the ground. Therefore, when in regalia, we often content ourselves with mutual shoulder touching and gentle brushing of hat brims.

Chapterette: A fellow member of the same Red Hat Society chapter.

Chocolate: A recognized food group by members of the Red Hat Society.

Disorganization: A Red Hat Society state of mind—there are no rules!

Elan: Vigorous spirit or enthusiasm.

Frivolous: Lacking in seriousness—perfectly acceptable in the Red Hat Society.

Gaudy: Ostentatiously ornamented, considered a good thing in Red Hat Society circles.

Hatiquette: The effort to be polite and aware of others when out in public as a group, despite sometimes raucous behavior.

Hatquarters: The offices of the Red Hat Society in Fullerton, California.

Hattitude: A fun, frivolous way of looking at life.

Hoots: An event that is unstructured and extremely informal and includes more than one chapter of the Red Hat Society.

Hysterian: Known in more boring organizations as a historian.

Kazoo: Official instrument of the Red Hat Society. Why? No. 1: It is an equal-opportunity instrument. Anyone can hum and play one. No. 2: It is eminently portable. No. 3: It is affordable. And No. 4: Group concerts are easily arranged.

Laugh: To show mirth or joy.

Let it Go!: A motto of the Red Hat Society usually screamed in public while waving a white napkin in the air.

Mirthday: The day on which a member celebrates the passage of another year. On this day, she reverses her colors and wears a purple hat and red clothing.

Pink Hatter: A wonderful woman who has not quite come of age but still cherishes the spirit of the Red Hat Society sisterhood.

Red Hatter: A fun-loving woman over the age of 50 who is also a member of the Red Hat Society.

Reduation: A ceremony during which a woman turning 50 is welcomed into the Red Hat Society.

Regalia: Those 50 and over must wear purple clothing and a red hat. Those under 50, fondly referred to as Pink Hatters, wear lavender clothing with pink hats.

Rocker: A Red Hatter who knows how to have fun; not to be confused with a chair that moves and is often used by the elderly.

Ruby RedHat: Mischievous mascot of the Red Hat Society.

Scarlet Sparkle: A story of something serendipitous that happens in the life of a Red Hatter. A magical connection that arises from the Red Hat Society.

The Wave: The official RHS greeting, performed by cupping the hand, fingers together, and ever-so-gently swiveling the wrist back and forth in the direction of the adoring throngs (or other Red Hatters).

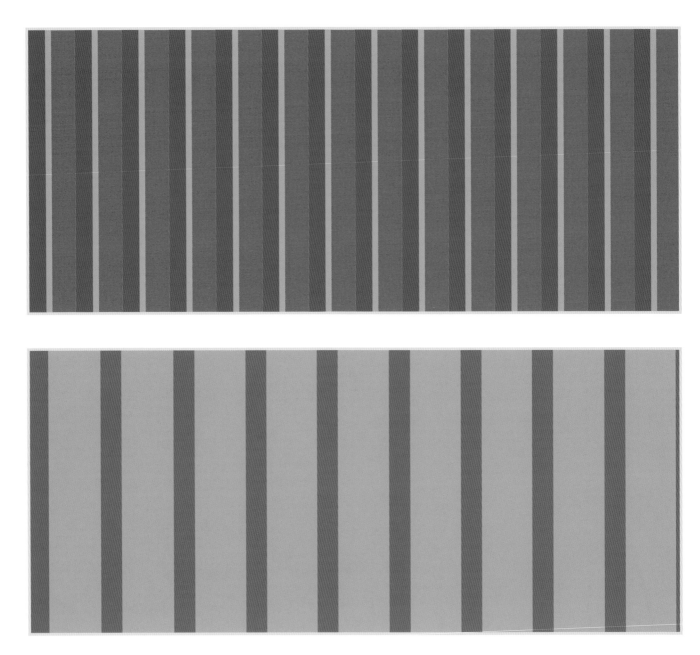

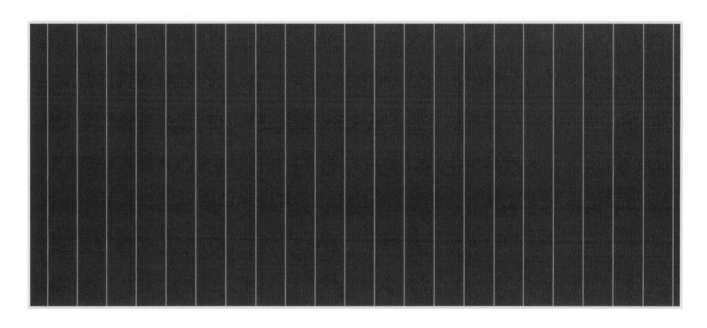

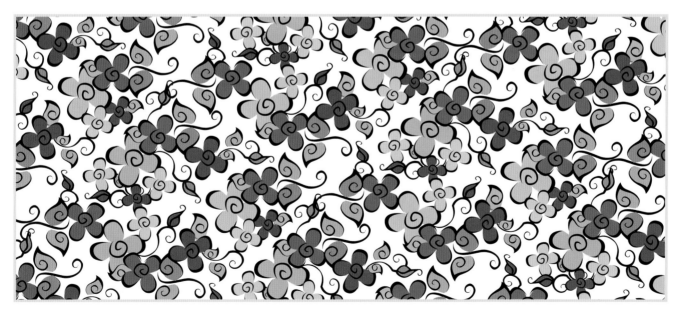

133

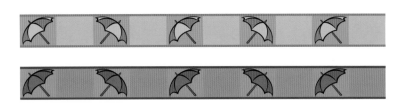

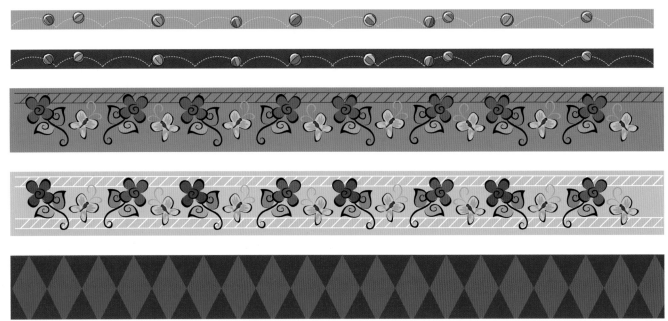

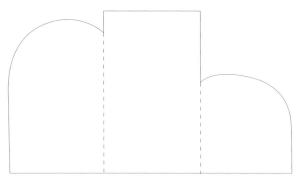

Congrats Flap Card Enlarge 400%

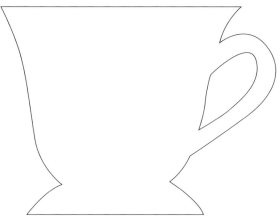

Teacup Card Enlarge 200%

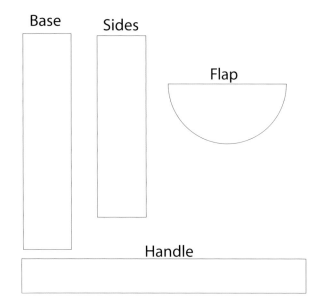

Base

Sides

Flap

Handle

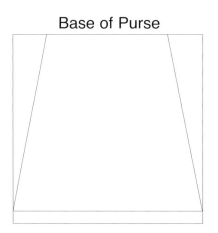

Base of Purse

Paper Purse Enlarge 400%

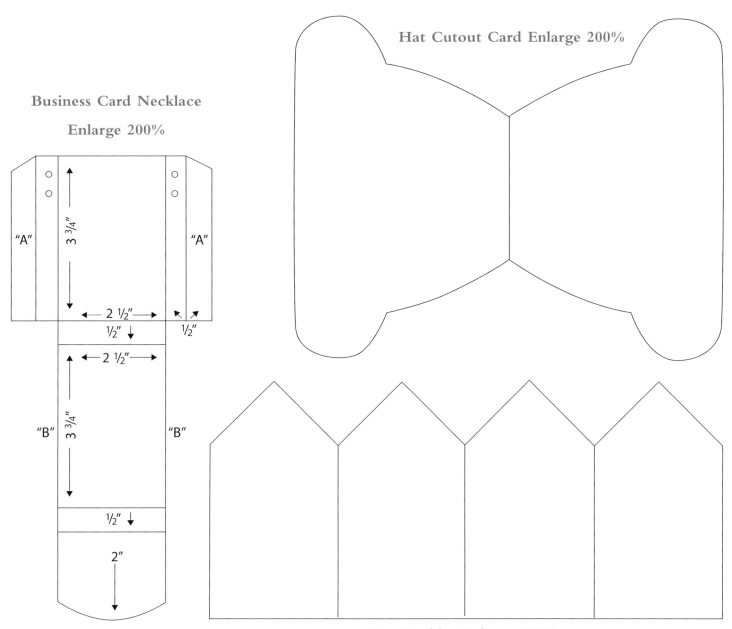

Hat Cutout Card Enlarge 200%

Business Card Necklace

Enlarge 200%

"A" "A"

3 ¾"

2 ½"

½" ↓   ½"

2 ½"

"B"   "B"

3 ¾"

½" ↓

2"

Tag Booklet Enlarge 200%

Teacup Door Hanger

Enlarge 200%

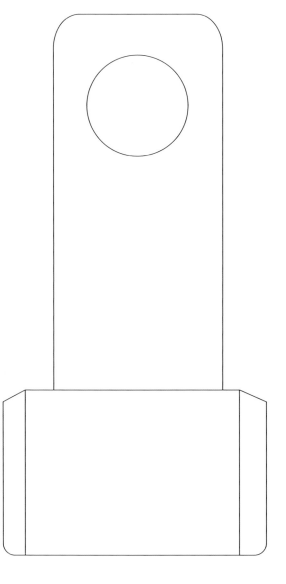

Tag template, copy to desired size

Tea Bag Card

Enlarge 200%

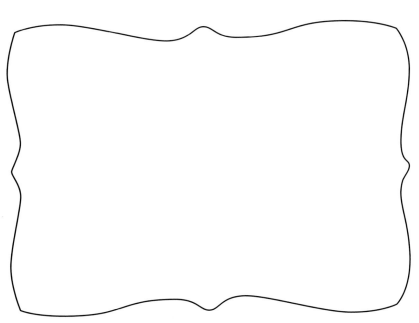

Frame

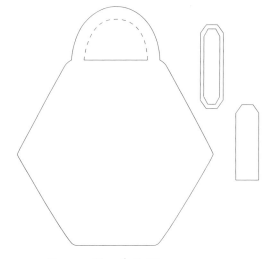

Purse Card & Tags

Enlarge 400%

So much
more than purple and red.

The Red Hat Society is an international "disorganization" of women who embrace the worth of deepening friendships and re-discovering the value of play. Underneath the frivolity, we share a bond of affection and a genuine enthusiasm for wherever life takes us next.

To learn more about the Red Hat Society:
www.redhatsociety.com

To request membership information by mail, please send your name, address and phone number to Red Hat Society Information Requests, P.O. Box 768, Fullerton, CA 92836.

There's Only One...
Join The Fun!™

Credits

A Red Lips 4 Courage Book
Red Lips 4 Courage
Communications, Inc.:
8502 E. Chapman Ave., 303
Orange, CA 92869
www.redlips4courage.com

Eileen Cannon Paulin,
Catherine Risling,
Rebecca Ittner, Jayne Cosh

Book Editor:
Eileen Cannon Paulin

Copy Editor:
Catherine Risling

Photo Stylist:
Rebecca Ittner

Book Designer:
Tony Olsen
Pinnacle Marketing
Ogden, UT

Photographers:
Denny Nelson
Zac Williams

Project Designer:
Jennifer Barber

Project Contributors:
Jill Bennett
Calley Crawford
Kara Johnson

Many of the paper products featured throughout this book are available at www.kandcompany.com. The tea service featured on page 22 is available at www.redhatsocietystore.com. A special thanks to Close to My Heart, www.closetomyheart.com.

Metric Equivalency Charts

inches to millimeters and centimeters

inches	mm	cm	inches	cm	inches	cm
⅛	3	0.3	9	22.9	30	76.2
¼	6	0.6	10	25.4	31	78.7
½	13	1.3	12	30.5	33	83.8
⅝	16	1.6	13	33.0	34	86.4
¾	19	1.9	14	35.6	35	88.9
⅞	22	2.2	15	38.1	36	91.4
1	25	2.5	16	40.6	37	94.0
1¼	32	3.2	17	43.2	38	96.5
1½	38	3.8	18	45.7	39	99.1
1¾	44	4.4	19	48.3	40	101.6
2	51	5.1	20	50.8	41	104.1
2½	64	6.4	21	53.3	42	106.7
3	76	7.6	22	55.9	43	109.2
3½	89	8.9	23	58.4	44	111.8
4	102	10.2	24	61.0	45	114.3
4½	114	11.4	25	63.5	46	116.8
5	127	12.7	26	66.0	47	119.4
6	152	15.2	27	68.6	48	121.9
7	178	17.8	28	71.1	49	124.5
8	203	20.3	29	73.7	50	127.0

yards to meters

yards	meters	yards	meters	yards	meters	yards	meters	yards	meters
⅛	0.11	2⅛	1.94	4⅛	3.77	6⅛	5.60	8⅛	7.43
⅛	0.11	2⅛	1.94	4⅛	3.77	6⅛	5.60	8⅛	7.43
¼	0.23	2¼	2.06	4¼	3.89	6¼	5.72	8¼	7.54
⅜	0.34	2⅜	2.17	4⅜	4.00	6⅜	5.83	8⅜	7.66
⅝	0.46	2½	2.29	4½	4.11	6½	5.94	8½	7.77
⅝	0.57	2⅝	2.40	4⅝	4.23	6⅝	6.06	8⅝	7.89
¾	0.69	2¾	2.51	4¾	4.34	6¾	6.17	8¾	8.00
⅞	0.80	2⅞	2.63	4⅞	4.46	6⅞	6.29	8⅞	8.12
1	0.91	3	2.74	5	4.57	7	6.40	9	8.23
1¼	1.03	3¼	2.86	5⅛	4.69	7¼	6.52	9⅛	8.34
1¼	1.14	3¼	2.97	5¼	4.80	7¼	6.63	9¼	8.46
1⅜	1.26	3⅜	3.09	5⅜	4.91	7⅜	6.74	9⅜	8.57
1½	1.37	3½	3.20	5½	5.03	7½	6.86	9½	8.69
1⅝	1.49	3⅝	3.31	5⅝	5.14	7⅝	6.97	9⅝	8.80
1¾	1.60	3¾	3.43	5¾	5.26	7¾	7.09	9¾	8.92
1⅞	1.71	3⅞	3.54	5⅞	5.37	7⅞	7.20	9⅞	9.03
2	1.83	4	3.66	6	5.49	8	7.32	10	9.14

Index